E YAM

PLAGUE
VILLAGE

EYAM
PLAGUE
VILLAGE

DAVID PAUL

AMBERLEY

First published 2012
Amberley Publishing
The Hill, Stroud
Gloucestershire, GL5 4EP

www.amberleybooks.com

British Library Cataloguing in Publication Data.
A catalogue record for this book is available from the British Library.

ISBN 978 1 4456 0396 4

Typesetting and Origination by Amberley Publishing.
Printed in Great Britain.

Contents

INTRODUCTION

Black Death first came to the shores of England in 1348/49. It is generally thought to have entered the country via the port of Melcombe Regis (Weymouth), having been brought over from Gascony; the disease first being reported in June of 1348. From there it quickly spread to Bristol and, by September of the same year, it had reached as far as London and East Anglia. By spring of 1349, the plague had travelled to Wales and the Midlands, and in 1350 it was taking its toll as far as the southern reaches of Scotland. Although accounts as to the number of deaths at that time differ, it is widely believed that between 25 per cent and 60 per cent of the country's population fell victim to the plague. There were several socio-economic consequences as a result of the pestilence; not least being the shortage of labour throughout the country. King Edward III was minded to introduce the Ordinance of Labourers, which fixed wages at pre-plague levels. This action, ultimately, precipitated the 'Peasants' Revolt' led by Wat Tyler.

Plague recurred on a national level at regular intervals, but, because of efforts made by central and local government from the late fifteenth century onwards, the effects of the plague were lessened as could be seen in the reduction in the death toll. Indeed, by the mid-seventeenth century, what was becoming known as the second pandemic was drawing to a close. During that time in the Great Plague of London (1665/66), an estimated 100,000 people, or 20 per cent of the population, died as a result of the plague. At its height, the plague was accounting for upwards of 7,000 deaths per week. It is also at that time that the small and somewhat isolated village of Eyam in Derbyshire was visited by the plague.

The Revd William Mompesson was rector of the parish of Eyam. He had been inducted into the parish in April 1664, following the death of the previous incumbent, the Revd Shoreland Adams. Mompesson, his wife Catherine, and their two children, George and Elizabeth, were settling into the parish when the plague arrived, inadvertently transported from London in a consignment of cloth destined for a local tailor.

George Viccars, thought to be a journeyman tailor, was lodging at the home of Alexander Hadfield. Viccars took delivery of a parcel of cloth and other materials. Upon finding the contents of the package to be damp, he was instructed to dry everything. It is thought that as he was drying the cloth in front of the fire, he was bitten by a flee carrying the deadly plague. He died on 7 September 1665, the plague's first victim. The disease soon spread to other people living in close proximity. During the initial months of the plague at Eyam, many of the more affluent and influential people living in the village were able to take refuge in other parts, but the vast majority of parishioners had to remain in their homes.

As the situation grew worse, the Revd Mompesson, in the absence of any other leading people in the village, came to the conclusion that he needed to take decisive action. Fearing that the contagion would spread to neighbouring towns and villages, the young rector, ably assisted by his puritan colleague, a former rector of the parish, the Revd Thomas Stanley, suggested that a number of measures should be taken in order to mitigate the effects of the plague. Following a meeting of villagers, it was agreed that there would be no funerals within the village, services of Divine Worship would be held away from the church, and finally, and most contentiously, a *cordon sanitaire* would encircle the village, and nobody would move outside of this prescribed area. The Earl of Devonshire, living a few miles away at Chatsworth House, was contacted, and agreed to supply provisions and medication at his own expense, providing that the *cordon sanitaire* was respected.

Even with the *cordon*'s boundaries being strictly adhered to, the disease continued unabated in the village itself, though many different plague remedies were being used. The rector's wife, Catherine Mompesson, worked tirelessly, carrying and dispensing remedies to those in need.

Catherine Mompesson pleaded with her husband to leave the parish with their two children until after the plague had departed. However, even given his wife's exhortations, the Revd Mompesson was resolute, accepting that it was his duty to remain with his parishioners, although he did implore her to take refuge in Sheffield with relatives. Catherine Mompesson would not leave her husband's side, but she did agree that their children should leave the parish for the duration of the plague's visitation.

Catherine Mompesson eventually fell victim to the plague herself, dying on 25 August 1666. The Revd William Mompesson was distraught and filled with grief, blaming himself for the death of his dear wife, by not having taken her advice to leave the parish.

Eyam: Plague Village is based upon events which actually took place during the time of the plague in Eyam. These are recorded in the chronological order in which they occurred. The diaries are fictional accounts as such, but letters and other official documents are recorded as they appear in extant records. Beth Hounsfeild and her husband, the Revd Edward Hounsfeild, are fictional characters.

The Wakes Festival as recorded in the text did take place during the summer of 1665. It is also reported that many more people than usual visited the festival that year, perhaps due the particularly fine weather which was being experienced during that summer. The Wakes vigil was disrupted for a short while, whilst 'dog whippers' cleared a young cow from the church. Catherine Mompesson had said at the time that it was an omen.

Although I have fictionalised many of the historical events, I have sought to retain the essence of known facts. For instance, Marshall Howe did perform the function of self-appointed plague sexton. The story of him carrying the 'corpse' of Edward Unwin is true. Unwin did recover after receiving the posset which he called for when being carried to his grave! Similarly, the case of the Bubnell carter and the Earl of Devonshire's personal physician is also true, as is the story of the woman from Orchard Bank who tried, unsuccessfully, to move to Tideswell at the height of the plague.

The sad case of Elizabeth Hancock is another true story. After burying her husband, John, and six of their children during the plague, it is thought that she fled to Sheffield; she was one of the few people to leave the village after the *cordon sanitaire* was agreed.

The plague remedies quoted at various points throughout the text were all used during the time of the pestilence, although just how effective they were is open to conjecture. One plague remedy which certainly was efficacious, was the prophylactic which Margaret Blackwell took – liquid fat from her brother's breakfast bacon! The story of Margaret Blackwell's remarkable recovery from the plague is still told in and around Eyam.

Various wills and letters are quoted throughout the text; all are truly recorded, using the English and spellings as documented. The chronology of the deaths in the text is as documented in official records.

During the course of my research I have visited the parish on many occasions and spoken to people in the village, but my primary sources of research, in addition to reading numerous texts and articles relating to the Plague at Eyam via the Internet, have been the excellent books by Clarence Daniels, *The Story of the Plague with a Guide to the Village*, and William Wood's highly acclaimed *The History and Antiquities of Eyam*.

Comments on the text are welcome at: davidpaul.eyam@gmail.com.

David Paul
24 August 2011

CHAPTER ONE
A Chance Discovery

My name is Cath Beaumont. I was christened after my grandmother's cousin, Catherine Mompesson. Following the tragic and lingering death of my grandmother last year, my parents were asked by my uncle, the sole executor of grandmother's will, to assist him in preparing her house for auction. As the furniture in the house was also being auctioned, they were requested to provide a complete inventory of any additional items that they wished to be entered in the auction. After grandfather's sudden death some years ago, grandmother moved back to the north of England to the bosom of her family. Up until that time, much of her married life had been spent in various rectories, as grandfather had taken holy orders following his time at Cambridge.

My parents spent many long days at the property but it was obvious from mother's gaunt and weary features that the task was proving to be very draining, both from a physical and emotional perspective. I gleaned from father's comments of exasperation and his irritable demeanour that he was not best pleased at being involved in the disposal of his mother-in-law's estate. It was therefore with evident and palpable relief that mother was pleased to accept my offer of help with the inventory. The following morning, shortly after breakfast, we set off on the three-mile journey to Garston, but the darkness was still holding to the trees in the Dam Wood giving the appearance of night rather than day. It was also unseasonably cold, as there was an icy mist rolling in off the Mersey; more reminiscent of winter than the tail end of summer. When we arrived we were greeted by my mother's brother, uncle Cedric, who'd journeyed from the neighbouring parish of Much Woolton. But there was little time to exchange pleasantries, as the auction was scheduled to be held sometime before the end of the month; so, while he and mother continued with the daunting task of cataloguing the furniture, I was allocated the role of collecting and collating the myriad sheaves of paper and other related items scattered throughout the extensive property. When I settled to my assignment it soon became apparent that much of the material was of limited interest, more often than not being receipts for purchases or household accounts, and only required a cursory glance.

As the day progressed, I worked steadily from one room to another, but found nothing of any significance. After lunch I spent some time looking through more papers in grandmother's bedroom. It was then that I stumbled across a large and elaborately carved camphor box. The box contained two small leather-bound notebooks, together with several bundles of papers, all of which were neatly tied together with blue silk ribbon. I failed to see any significance in the colour of the ribbons and perhaps there was none. I didn't bother to undo any of the papers but instead concentrated on emptying the contents of the box, as I thought it may prove useful for storing some of my own correspondence. It was only when a loose letter fell from between the bundles that my interest became aroused. Here was a connection with the past, which both intrigued and fascinated me. In a strange way, there was something very mysterious about it.

Deciding to stop for a well-earned rest, I sat in a window seat, which gave more access to daylight, and allowed me to read the letter without having to search for a candle. The letter, which was addressed to my grandmother, was written in the hand of my namesake, her cousin, Mrs Catherine Mompesson. Dated Tuesday 4 July 1665, over forty years ago, the letter invited her and my grandfather over to Eyam for a few weeks. The purpose of the visit was to renew their acquaintance, after having not seen one another for some time, and to attend and enjoy the Wakes Festival.

The letter read as follows:

Eyam Rectory
Eyam
High Peak
Derbyshire

Tuesday 4 July 1665

To my dearest cousin Beth,

I trust that this letter finds you and your dear husband, Edward, well; you are both often in our thoughts and prayers. There's so much that has been happening in the parish, it's difficult to know exactly where to begin. Our babes, George and Elizabeth are now growing into fit and healthy young children and my health is much improved since we left Scalby, near Scarborough, although I cannot think why as the winter here in High Peak is every bit as inclement as near the coast and the winds certainly appear to be just as fierce – if not more so!

Since William's induction, which now seems so long ago although, in truth, it was somewhat less than eighteen months ago, much has happened in the parish. Perhaps it's unworthy to speak of the dead, but I have gathered from talking to some of the parishioners, that the former rector of the parish, the Revd Shoreland Adams, was not too well thought of here, choosing to spend much of his time at his other living at Treeton in Yorkshire. As you may know, he died in April of last year, leaving a wife and nine children. In one respect, perhaps because of the antipathy towards the Revd Shoreland Adams, William has been welcomed into the parish by many of the parishioners. But conversely, because of the fact that the former and much-loved Puritan rector, the Revd Thomas Stanley, has now returned to live in the parish following the death of his dear wife in June last year, it's proving difficult for William to be accepted by all of the people of the village, as some still harbour Puritan leanings, albeit dormant or concealed. Also, William is many years younger than the Revd Stanley, and I believe that this engenders a certain degree of reticence.

But enough of these dismal and depressing thoughts, and on to my main reason for writing to you at this time. It seems so long since we have met that William thought that both of you may wish to spend a few weeks over here with us, especially as we're now nearing the time of the Wakes Festival. It's always a joyous occasion; the village grows out of all proportion, with many relatives and friends coming from near and far to join in the festivities. This year, as the weather has been so good of late, it promises to be particularly momentous. You may not be familiar with all of the customs and traditions which are observed over here in Derbyshire, they're certainly very different from those we enjoyed over in Yorkshire, and I'm sure that there may be even greater differences from the festivals held over in Lancashire.

As William graduated from Peterhouse a couple of years before Edward, I know that he'd be very interested in finding out what's happened in the college since he moved away. I'm sure that they'll have many similar memories of such an old and well established college. William was telling me the other day, with a certain amount of pride I have to report, that Peterhouse is the oldest college in Cambridge; just another fact of which I was totally ignorant.

I told our babes, George and Elizabeth, that you might be coming over to stay with us here at the rectory, but I'm not sure that they fully understood exactly what I was saying, although they appeared to be overjoyed, only ever hearing about you, but never actually having seen you. I do so hope that you and Edward will be able to come over to share some time with us. The Wakes actually starts on St Helen's Day, which is 18 August, but the festival period will continue into the following week. If you are able to join us, could I suggest that you aim to arrive, say, sometime during the week beginning Monday 31 July, but we'd be pleased to welcome you at any time to suit your convenience and commitments.

Please give Edward my warmest good wishes.

I am and will always remain your loving cousin
Catherine

Many thoughts were evoked while reading the letter; it certainly stirred my natural curiosity and I was anxious to ascertain if grandmother had responded. I searched diligently through the papers, undoing every single bundle, but failed to find any evidence of my grandmother having responding to her cousin's letter. Although I'd been given the task of sorting out all of the papers in the house, I nonetheless felt a slight twinge of guilt when reading through the many bundles, which were the personal recollections of my grandmother's time at Eyam. It was obvious from reading her notes that she had replied, and the notes themselves revealed a far more sinister and distressing sequence of events. But I still couldn't find the letter that she'd sent back to her cousin. The only avenue left to explore was to read through the notebooks. As soon as I opened the first book, I found the letter in question, tucked inside the back cover. The letter read as follows:

Smithy Cottage
The Lane
Dungeon
in the county of Lancashire

Monday 17 July 1665

Dearest cousin Catherine,

Thank you for your most welcome letter which I received towards the end of last week. We would be very happy to travel over to Eyam to share with you the excitement of the Wakes festivities. As you say, it will no doubt be very different from the type of festival that we traditionally hold over here in Lancashire but I'm sure that that will add to the pleasure. Both Edward and I are very much looking forward to seeing you and William again, and we are thrilled with the prospect of meeting for the first time your darling children George and Elizabeth. I have delayed writing until now because, since that time, Edward has been looking at the travel arrangements for us. I own to not appreciating the complexity of arranging to travel such a great distance. We haven't been able to finalise the arrangements as yet, but Edward is of the opinion that there's a possibility that we might be able to travel to Lyme Handley which is quite near to Disley, where one of his old friends from Cambridge is rector. We could possibly break our journey there and then, following that, travel on to Eyam. Accordingly, he has written to his friend, to request a visit. If arrangements go as planned, we would be hoping to arrive in Eyam sometime towards the end of the week, maybe on Thursday 3 August, or possibly Friday 4 August.

I'm so excited at the prospect of visiting Eyam, so I trust that Edward will be able to finalise our travel arrangements in the near future. Incidentally, Edward says that there have been a number of developments at Peterhouse, many of which are connected to the recent Act of Uniformity, and the new Book of Common Prayer. I'm sure that Edward and William will spend much time discussing ecclesiastical and political matters, as is always the way when clergymen meet.

I will end this letter now, in the hope of greeting you and your dear family in the near future.

I remain, as always, your loving cousin
Beth

I felt in a very strange state when I finished reading; on the one hand wanting to determine, from the contemporaneous documents which were now in my possession, exactly what had happened between my forebears all those years ago, and conversely wishing to maintain the inviolable sanctity of their innermost thoughts.

I took the bundles of papers and the notebooks home that evening. Over the next few weeks I read and re-read every page in the two notebooks, finding it increasingly difficult to comprehend and even contemplate the dreadful truth which they contained. The notebooks were the diaries of my grandmother's cousin, and dated from a time immediately prior to the Wakes festivities of 1665, right through to the time of her becoming possessed of the plague in August 1666; the last diary entry being 22 August 1666.

The bundles of papers were notes written by my grandmother and covered the period from my grandparents setting out on their ill-fated journey from Lancashire on 1 August 1665, until their return in November 1666 – significantly longer than they had originally envisaged.

I pieced the material together into some sort of chronological order, interspersing grandmother's notes between pages from her cousin's diary – they painted a depressing and alarming, but totally courageous and selfless picture of the part which they played during the tragedy that befell the tiny village, almost half a century ago. There were, however, a number of gaps in the information which I gleaned from the diaries and papers. At this point mother contacted a distant relative in Derbyshire and, after a somewhat long and protracted correspondence, I was able to secure a copy of the journal of my forebear, the Revd William Mompesson, the husband of my grandmother's cousin. I was given permission to use extracts from his journal for the period in question, thus giving context and depth to the material that I already possessed. But, I have to record that certain extracts from his journal may give the appearance of being somewhat direct and terse. However, given the constant strain under which he and his colleague, the Revd Thomas Stanley, were working during that unprecedented period, it is perhaps understandable why his thoughts are recorded in such a forthright manner. One thing is however evident, and that is that they are a totally honest record of the happenings in the village at that time.

Since collating these various notes, written principally by my grandmother, her cousin and her cousin's husband, I have had the opportunity of visiting the village for myself. During that visit I was able to retrace the steps which were so familiar to my grandmother and her cousin. The walks evoked vicarious memories which I'll treasure for many years.

In presenting this account of the terrible events which took place in Eyam during the latter part of 1665 and most of 1666, I have used, exclusively, as stated, grandmother's notes and relevant entries from her cousin's diary. I have not written any of the account in my own hand, nor have I added to or detracted from any of the collated material. Where the notes and diaries proved to be short in factual detail, I have used extracts from the more formally written journal of the Revd William Mompesson; the husband of my grandmother's cousin, and the man, claimed by many, to be the 'saviour' of Eyam during the visitation of the plague. But, having now had time to read at length and digest all of the relevant documents and assorted papers, I have come to the considered opinion that the Revd Thomas Stanley, a fellow worker with the Revd William Mompesson, should be accorded an equal share of praise for his tireless efforts during that terrible time. But, perhaps it's not for me to judge. I can only suggest that the readers of these assembled notes form their own judgements, as I have been able to do.

Cath Beaumont
Lovel Hall
Speke Village,
in the county of Lancashire

Monday 20 August 1706

CHAPTER TWO
Eyam Wakes

From the hand of Beth Hounsfeild:
Friday 4 August 1665

We had intended to leave the village on Monday morning but, because of parochial duties which Edward was obliged to fulfil and also some particularly inclement weather for the time of the year, it was decided that we would leave for Eyam early on Tuesday. Fortunately the weather was much better as we left the village, although the tracks were still a little muddy as we headed towards the village of Cronton where we rested for some little while at the Unicorn Inn on the drovers' road. Later in the morning, we made our way to Great Sankey, and then on through the village of Grappenhall, arriving in the parish of Lymm in the Bucklow Hundred later in the afternoon. After such a wearisome day, we stopped and stayed overnight at the Bear's Paw – a hostelry on the outskirts of the small village. Some of the unsavoury characters and labourers who visited the tavern later that evening were very boisterous and loud, and I fear a little taken in strong drink, so Edward and I retired to our chamber somewhat earlier than anticipated. This also meant that we could make an early start the following morning.

Our breakfast on Wednesday was very wholesome, which was different from what we had anticipated in this small village tavern. We travelled as far as Bowden in the morning and stopped for lunch, someway between there and Bramhall. Once again it was late afternoon before we arrived at Lyme Handley which is a small township in Prestbury Parish. We were due to stay for the night with one of Edward's colleagues from his days at St Peter's College. We were indeed made most welcome by the Revd Grisedale who is rector of one of the smaller parishes in the Macclesfield Hundred, encompassing the hamlets of Middlecote, Pott Wood and Sponds.

We had expected to leave for Eyam on Thursday, but the Revd Grisedale asked us to stay for another evening, as he had invited the rector from the neighbouring parish over to dinner – he too was a St Peter's man, but had graduated many years before either Edward or the Revd Grisedale.

So, it wasn't until this morning that we left the rectory to make our way over to Eyam. The lanes outside of the villages were not too well maintained or defined, even though responsibility for roads had been transferred from the manor to the parishes. Our progress was slow. Indeed, the journey from Lyme Handley to Whaley Bridge took us much longer than Edward had predicted, and then we had to travel through Chapel-en-le-Frith, but Edward said that we needed to make progress if we were to arrive at Eyam at not too late an hour. We took the road towards Tideswell, which was better than some which we had travelled along, and having passed through there it was but a relatively short journey on to Eyam itself.

Catherine and her husband, William, were effusive in their greetings, although Catherine was somehow different from the way in which I had remembered her. The blush-rose glow in her cheeks had now surrendered to a sallow eggshell-like complexion, but she still had the same vivacity which I well recollected.

Both William and Catherine appreciated that we were weary after our long and, at times, hazardous journey from Speke. Dungeon and Speke now seem a very great distance away. After dinner Catherine and I did speak for a short while but Edward and William must have become engrossed in their conversation, as Edward did not retire to our chamber until much later.

Our tiny hamlet of Dungeon looks so very different from what little that we've seen of the village here at Eyam. I'm looking forward to spending some time with Catherine's children tomorrow.

Extract from the Journal of the Revd William Mompesson:
Friday 4 August 1665

We welcomed Beth and her husband, Edward, to the rectory today, albeit somewhat later than we had anticipated – however, it was good to see them, especially after their long and somewhat tortuous journey from Lancashire. After resting for a little while and being shown their bed chamber, we ate our evening meal together although they were clearly weary from the journey. While Catherine and her cousin remained in the dining room, talking no doubt of family matters, I retired to the study with Edward. Catherine had informed me that he was a Peterhouse man, but he went up to Cambridge some years after I'd actually left. Initially, we talked of their hazardous journey to the village. Edward expressed some surprise at how rough the narrow tracks were into the village, and how remote the village itself was, being in a more isolated location than he had envisaged. Apparently, it was very different from their dwelling in the hamlet of Dungeon, near to the village of Speke in Lancashire.

Edward, being a Classics scholar, found the early history of Eyam and its importance during the Roman occupation captivating – especially when I said that there was a settlement on this very site in the early part of the Bronze Age. I suggested to him that perhaps after the Wakes Festival we could venture to the village of Brough-on-Noe, about five miles to the north-west of the parish, and here see the remains of the fort of Navio. The fort was of strategic importance to the Romans, in that it protected their interests in the lead mining industry which was centred in and around Eyam. It also served to safeguard the lines of communication to the fort and settlement of Aquae Arnemetiae, the spa town which we now know as Buxton.

We then went on to talk about the village's Anglian stone cross in which Edward had shown interest. I mentioned the fact that it is believed to date from the late eighth century, and was thought to have been a 'preaching cross', around which people from local villages and hamlets would gather for Divine Worship before a church was established. The village of Eyam itself was established in Anglo-Saxon times. Aiune, which is one of the earlier spellings of its name, is a Saxon word and means 'a settlement by the water', although others have suggested that it means 'land between two streams' as the village does indeed stand on a shale promontory, below the gritstone of Eyam Edge and above the limestone of Middleton Dale, between the valleys of the Hollow Brook and Jumber Brook. As I went on to tell Edward; the abundance of water in the vicinity was, together with the plentiful reserves of lead, the main reason for the founding of the village. Sometime during the fifteenth century, the village name was written Eyham or Eham, but now it is universally known as Eyam. I also told Edward of the tiny hamlet of Bretton which lies within the parish and is located a little north of the village. Like Eyam, its ancient name is of great significance, meaning mountainous. I suggested that we might walk there one day; but, as the candles were now guttering, we agreed that it was time to end our conversation and retire for the night.

From the Diary of Catherine Mompesson:
Saturday 5 August 1665

Beth still looked a little tired at breakfast this morning but, nonetheless, I suggested that in order to blow the cobwebs away it might be an idea for us to have a short walk around the village and, in that way, we could renew our acquaintance. When we were younger, I met with Beth far more than I have latterly and certainly since both of us married. When William and I attended Beth and Edward's wedding neither of our children were born, so it will be good for them to meet their second cousin later this morning – both of them having gone to bed shortly after Beth and Edward's arrival last night. We only walked as far as Townend, and I told Beth some of the history and traditions of the village before the Wakes Festival.

As we walked I mentioned that our parish is in the Honours of Peveril and Tutbury; in the ecclesiastical jurisdiction of the Archdeaconry of Derby, and in the Diocese of Lichfield and Coventry. The village itself stands in the south-east part of the parish, and is about six miles from our nearest town which is Bakewell. I told Beth of the market which is held in the town every Monday, and said that I'd visited on a few occasions, whenever there was a wagon going over that way.

Beth made reference to the fact that the houses and cottages looked very neat and tidy. I said that some of it was in preparation for the Wakes Festival but that the houses were generally in very good repair, as most of the parishioners were gainfully employed in agriculture, lead mining or often a combination of both.

I told Beth that the boundaries of the parish are such to make it nearly circular, and that they encompass the townships of Foolow and Woodland Eyam. The hamlets of Bretton and Hazelford also lie within the bounds of the parish and I suggested that we could make the short walk over to Bretton sometime in the coming days. On a more general note, I mentioned that our parish lies between the parishes of Hope, Hathersage and Bakewell – and that William and I have beaten the bounds, starting at the rivulet which runs close to Stoney Middleton Churchyard. Beth shewed much interest so I continued by saying that, from there, we walked to the top of Stoke Wood and then along Goatcliffe Brook. The boundary then follows the River Derwent, Highlow Brook and continues to the top of Grindlow. After Wardlow Mires it is but a short step to Foundley fence, then to Dale Brook and finally back to the rivulet where we first started. Again, I suggested that we could walk the bounds some time after the Wakes Festival.

I could see that Beth was enjoying our walk and also absorbing the prettiness of the village. I told her that from my very first day in the village I too was captivated by its sheer beauty, which is quite varied and very picturesque. As we walked towards Townend many of the cottages were covered in variegated ivy and there was an abundance of fruit trees, together with a number of large sycamore trees along the edge of the street. As well as the numerous cottages we passed, I drew Beth's attention to the many solidly-built mansions which equalled in grandeur any that either of us had ever seen elsewhere. She then made reference to the constant activity in the numerous beehives along the way, with the coming and going of countless honey bees.

Continuing on our way, we ventured northwards from the village at a steady pace to a mountain range and Beth was clearly surprised to find that it scaled heights of almost 600 feet. The hillsides there are crowned with tree plantations, which I believe have the added advantage of warding off the chill winds which blow as winter takes its grip on the village. Looking down from our vantage point, the village below us looked calm and peaceful – truly, a sight to behold.

I said that further to the east out of the village is Riley Wood which rises on a steep slope, although we wouldn't venture that far today. Some way from the wood is Riley farm, where the Hancocks and Talbots live. William has visited both families on a number of occasions but I've only ever seen them when they've come into the village to sell eggs or butter; they very rarely attend Divine Worship. Further over still is the village of Stoney Middleton, a third part of that village is also included within the bounds of our parish.

To the south of the village, which may be a walk for another day, two dells run parallel into Middleton Dale. The Delf, or Delve as it is called by some of the older parishioners, is very secluded and a very beautiful place to walk on a summer's afternoon, especially when the flowers are blooming in profusion and the birds are singing in the oak and chestnut trees. Towards the western end of the dell, there is Salt Pan; an unusual name and nobody in the village knows from whence it came. A stream issues from among the limestone, and gently winds its way through a shallow bed of moss, ferns, foxglove and water mint. Eyam Dale, the other dell, is also rich in its rural beauty with towering grey rocks on one side and a rising wood on the other. This, in turn, leads to the place called the 'Rock Garden', a well-known meeting place for courting couples.

Beth was obviously pleased to hear of the areas surrounding the village but, having walked some considerable distance for one morning, we turned and started to make our way back and there, standing at the village's centre as a timeless reminder of stability and strength, were the dominant lines of the parish church.

From the hand of Beth Hounsfeild:
Saturday 5 August 1665

As the weather was particularly fine this morning, Catherine suggested that we should go for a short walk around the village following breakfast although, truth to tell, I was still feeling somewhat weary after our long journey from Lancashire. Leaving the rectory we walked towards the eastern side of the village, the area is known as Townend, and here we saw the Lydgate – which Catherine said was very interesting and so told me all about it. We also passed the bull ring on our way to Water Lane but I wasn't too interested in that, especially when Catherine told me what went on there. Over towards the western side of the village is the area known as the Town Head and Catherine said that we could walk over that way on another occasion. In fact, the church, whose patron saint is St Helen, is located at the mid-point of the village and the church grounds have a number of linden trees. We then walked out of the village, through a densely covered plantation, and up the hill. As we stood on the top and overlooked the parish, both of us beheld the beauty and majesty in God's creation in the village below. However, it must have been quite obvious to Catherine that I was somewhat jaded, as she suggested that we should make our way back to the church, where we could rest, and she would tell me some of the geography and history of the village.

Catherine said that the village itself is, in essence, one long street of nearly a mile in length. And, perhaps uniquely, houses built on the north side of the street (which runs from east to west) stand on shale and sandstone while those built on the south side of the street are built mostly on limestone. This pattern is constant for the entire length of the street. The street, and for that matter the village, can be divided into three distinctive parts. Towards the eastern end of the village is the area known as the Townend – that's the part of the village from which we'd just returned. A number of roads lead from here, including the Lydgate, Water Lane, the Dale and the Cocey or Causeway. Right in the very centre of the village is the church and the rectory, and then, at the western extremity of the village there is the Townhead. Catherine also told me about Riley Wood and Stoney Middleton, but we didn't venture that far today.

As we were making our way back, I gathered from Catherine's oblique questions that she was intrigued to know the substance of the long conversation which Edward and William had shared after dinner last night. I confessed that I was as ignorant as she, but surmised that it might have related to Edward's search for a living in either Lancashire or Cheshire. As Catherine had only met Edward on one previous occasion, we went on to talk of events immediately prior to and following his graduation. I told her that, shortly after leaving Cambridge, he moved back to his roots in the north of England and we were married, which was, of course, when he and Catherine had first made each other's acquaintance. It was after our marriage that we moved to the hamlet of Dungeon, by the small village of Speke, on the banks of the River Mersey. I don't believe that Catherine is familiar with the geography of the area, just like I was unaware of the area around Eyam, but I informed her that the village lies near to the parish of Hale where one of Edward's mentors, the Revd Samuel Ellison, is rector. We have lived here for eight months now. Edward is heavily involved in parish matters in Hale and I spend much of my time with the women-folk in Speke, Dungeon and Oglet. Our dwelling, which is on farm land owned by the rector, lies towards the end of Dungeon Lane, close to the river bank.

Edward and William were still making visits around the parish when we returned to the rectory. I'm already forming the impression that William would be happy to have Edward stay in the parish and become his curate; but these are early days as yet.

From the hand of Beth Hounsfeild:
Tuesday 15 August 1665

Preparations for the forthcoming Wakestide celebrations are progressing well. Everyone in the parish is looking forward to welcoming family and friends back into the village. During these last weeks, both Catherine and William have been very involved in the final preparations but, today, Catherine said that she would put some time aside in order to show me a little more of the village and the church. Since we arrived, almost two weeks ago now, there has been very little time for us to renew our acquaintance, what with one thing or another; but today we're going to have another walk around the village and also spend a little time in the parish church.

As we walked from the rectory in the direction of The Square, Catherine remarked that the sky was a Cambridge blue. It was an odd phrase and one which I hadn't heard before, although she said that William often described the sky as such – no doubt a throwback to his time at Peterhouse. But Edward, also a graduate of Peterhouse, had never described the heavens in such terms. We stopped when we arrived at Lydgate and Catherine explained that Lyd is a Saxon word which means 'to cover or protect' and it was here that, every night, the gate sealed off the village and 'watch and ward' is kept from nine o'clock until six the following morning. Every able-bodied man who is a householder in the village is required to take his turn on the rota. The watchman, whose duty it is to maintain the security of the parish, is required to question anyone seeking admittance into the village and raise the alarm if danger threatens during the hours of darkness. During the watch he carries a lantern and a large wooden halbert or 'watch-bill', which is there to act as protection. At the end of the watch, the lantern and 'watch-bill' are placed outside the door of his successor. Although we'd visited this area of the village just the other day, Catherine hadn't explained to me the significance of the place.

We turned and walked back towards the church, which Catherine said also dated from Saxon times. Upon entering, she pointed out the two pillars between the nave and north aisle which she said are of Norman origin, but which rest upon Saxon bases. Catherine mentioned that, since their arrival in the parish, she had spent some time with the wardens and had learnt much about the church's history. She went on to explain that the windows of the bell chamber in the tower, the pointed arches on each side of the nave, the capitals of the pillars and the archway into the tower, are all of the Decorated period. We then made our way to the small doorway in the west wall of the tower which, I was informed, also dates from this period. Before leaving the church, we went over to the south side of the chancel, which is lighted by three lancet windows of the Early English period. Over on the west end of the north aisle are two others of Decorated design.

Coming from the church before making our way to the part of the village known as The Cross, we met William who was standing, deep in thought, in the churchyard. He accompanied us to the shuttered building which is known as the market house. It is from here that farmers congregate to sell butter, eggs and poultry to the villagers; the market cross also stands on this site. William said that on the verge of the drovers' road, which runs between Sheffield and Manchester, there is a Saxon cross which has stood for over a thousand years and has carved-vine scrolled and interlaced knotwork. He also informed us that, as recently as 1643, it had escaped being totally destroyed when Puritan zealots, with the authorisation of an Act of Parliament, were empowered to remove and destroy 'all crosses in any open place'.

This evening, the Revd John Walker (Vicar of Hathersage) joined us for dinner. He is a good friend of William's.

From the hand of Beth Hounsfeild:
Monday 21 August 1665

After the Wakes Vigil yesterday, which most of the parishioners attended at some time, the morning of the Wakes Festival itself dawned to an air of eager anticipation. I was awakened by the sounds of heightened activity in the village drifting through the mullioned windows of the bedroom – the clatter and banging as preparations were made for the forthcoming festival and the alarm calls of the birds in the trees around the rectory, unaccustomed as they were to the unusual flurry of morning activity.

The everyday sounds of the rectory coming to life for another day were also somewhat different from the norm, suggesting that here too there was a different emphasis being placed upon the morning's routines; even the creaking of the bare wooden floorboards seemed more frenetic as the maid went about her early morning duties. Both Edward and I had been looking forward to this day ever since Catherine had written to me, some many months ago now. During the week we'd watched as preparations for the festival were being made, which involved, amongst other things, cleaning dwellings from top to bottom and many cottages in the village being newly white-washed especially for the occasion.

The celebrations started early in the morning and, almost as soon as we left the rectory after breaking our fast, we encountered a vile stink of ale and even scenes of drunken behaviour, as we walked past the King's Head, but Catherine assured me that this was but a small part of the celebrations which parishioners and their families and friends enjoyed on this day. She acknowledged that public houses in and around the village did brisk business at this time, but continued by saying that it was merely to affirm peoples' joyfulness on such a happy day. It was amazing to see the village swelled with so many people; far more than had ever visited before, according to Catherine's estimate. Earlier we'd witnessed what, to my mind, was a truly barbaric scene: the so-called sport of Goose Riding. During this spectacle, which many parishioners avoided, a goose was suspended, by its legs, from a rope that had been tied across the main street. As the goose was swinging in the air, a succession of mainly younger people rode, one at a time, at full speed under the rope, with the aim of pulling off the goose's head; the neck having previously been greased. Apparently, it was a skilled accomplishment to be successful in this sport, being an activity more suited to experienced horsemen. Catherine told me that there was always much betting on the competitors in the event; either for money or for a quantity of ale. The prize to the successful contestant was the goose itself. It was not unknown in the district for similar goose riding events to be held on Shrove Tuesday and Easter Monday.

In light of my displeasure at witnessing that event, Catherine suggested that it might be better if we avoided the cock fighting and bull baiting, which would be taking place further up the village, as these too were somewhat barbarous events. Perhaps in mitigation, she said that many people believed that the act of bull baiting actually improved the flavour of the meat when the bull was slaughtered, adding that in places such as Chesterfield there was, she thought, a bye-law which forbade butchers from slaughtering animals which hadn't been baited. The bull was chained by either its leg or neck, and then tormented by dogs which were trained to pin it down by the nose; it was considered that this area was particularly tender. Because of the popularity and necessity of bull baiting, there was another bull ring by the village cross in Foolow, just a mile or so from the village, and there were two bull rings at Tideswell.

We spent a little more time looking around the village at the Wakes activities and talking with parishioners, before turning to make our, now wearisome, way back to the rectory; but before arriving we stopped at the village green where many of the young people of the village, together with some of their younger relatives, had assembled to take part in the dancing which is an integral and traditional part of the Wakes Festival. Catherine commented again on the number of relatives and friends from outside of the village who had made their way to the Wakes this year. She'd been told by many parishioners that there were far more people visiting this year than ever – perhaps it was due to the very warm weather that we're enjoying at the moment.

After returning to the rectory we found that William and Edward were still out somewhere in the village, enjoying the last few hours of the festival. I took the opportunity of broaching the subject of our return to Lancashire. Catherine insisted that, because Edward and William were finding so much that they held in common, we should delay our return for a few weeks and continue to enjoy the unusually warm summer which they are experiencing in the Peaks this year.

I retired to bed that evening feeling totally exhausted, but totally exhilarated by the events of the day.

From the Diary of Catherine Mompesson:
Monday 21 August 1665

There was an incident at Divine Service yesterday which, I know, troubled William greatly. Some way through the Wake, which had been attended by a great many of the parishioners, a number of youths (perhaps being taken in drink, although I couldn't vouchsafe for this) had driven a young cow into the church. This profane act defiled the sanctity of the service but fortunately the churchwardens, who also acted as official 'dog whippers', removed the now terrified calf from the church and we were able to continue. The whole incident upset me, it was as though it was a portent of something, but I know not what.

Fortunately, this morning broke to happier sounds coming from the village and I looked forward to enjoying the Wakes Festival, together with the relatives and friends of the villagers. This was the second Wakes Festival that we've witnessed since William was inducted into the living last April; but this year was extra special because of the visit of my cousin

Beth and her husband, Edward, in whom William has immediately found a kindred spirit.

During the day we witnessed some overly exuberant behaviour, with which I believe Beth viewed with some distain, but, generally speaking, we both enjoyed the day immensely, especially the dancing which we watched immediately before returning to the rectory in the early evening. As we talked before William and Edward returned, Beth mentioned that they should be returning to Lancashire in the near future but I tried to persuade her that they should stay a few weeks longer, especially as William and Edward obviously had so many shared interests and experiences. Judging by what looked to me as a conspiratorial smile which lightened across her visage, I believe that this suggestion might have received her tacit agreement; we'll discuss it at more length tomorrow.

From the hand of Beth Hounsfeild:
Tuesday 22 August 1665

After the excitement of yesterday's festival, Catherine suggested that we might stay in the rectory this morning and collect our wits. We sat drinking tea whilst Mrs Elizabeth Abell, a recently married parishioner, gave us further information relating to some more of the customs and traditions of the village. She told us that when the curfew bell is rung every evening, as darkness falls, its main purpose is to guide men working out of the village or other travellers safely back to the parish – especially when inclement weather makes it difficult to follow outlying pathways. The curfew bell was also, in days now gone, a signal for people inside the village to extinguish any fires at the end of the day, so as to help prevent any accidental fires. But the curfew bell had other important purposes; after ringing the curfew, in order to let villagers know the day of the month, the bell is tolled the requisite number of times – once for every day of that month. Also, the bell is tolled whenever anyone in the village has died – twice for a woman and three times for a man. The bell is then tolled again when the body is taken into the church for the burial service. It was Catherine who then recalled one of the traditions which often occurs on the day of interment, whereby relatives, friends and neighbours of the deceased are invited to a special dinner called the Arthel, or Arvel, dinner. Its origins apparently relate to the time, many years ago, when the corpse was publicly exposed immediately before burial, thereby exculpating the inheritors of the deceased's land and property from any charge of foul play. Also on these occasions, relatives of the deceased provide biscuits for the mourners to take away. It was a custom which she knew was practised in many towns and villages, and one which she had also been familiar with in their previous parish. Mrs Abell then said that the tradition of Lich-waking, was still practised by some of the older and wealthier families in the village, whereby relatives sat by the deceased's body both night and day until the day of interment. Another tradition, which Mrs Abell said is still observed in the village, is the custom of clay daubing, whereby friends and family of a newly married couple get together, directly after the wedding, and build them a dwelling cottage. The technique of wattle-and-clay daubing is directed by a man called the dauber. When the work is completed, usually on the same day as starting, there is more merrymaking and festivities. I found the whole conversation very enlightening as nothing of this nature, to the best of my knowledge, happens either in Lancashire or Cheshire. When I related the details of this particular custom to Edward later that evening, he told me that he'd heard that it was a tradition practised in certain parts of Brittany; notably in the areas around Guingamp and Morlaix, which he'd visited during his days at Cambridge.

Before taking her leave, Mrs Abell had related two more of the many traditions of Eyam, one being so old that originally it was thought to be one of the incantations practised at festivals of the Druids. During the ceremony the forehead of a sick person is anointed with May dew; the May dew having been carefully gathered at daybreak. This remedy is considered to be very effective. Another ceremony, which can also be traced directly to the Druids, consisted in carrying long poles of mountain ash festooned with flowers at May Day celebrations, together with the hanging of bunches of flowers from cottage windows. Mrs Abell ended by talking of the practice of putting the coffin of a young person, with the deceased in it, on the bed with the bed clothes spread over it in such a way that it looked as though the dead person was in a gentle sleep. The tradition was meant to signify that the innocent and beautiful youth would be awakened, as from sleep, to immortality and light – truly a charming, if not wholly Christian, custom.

After Mrs Abell had gone, I remembered the incident which had happened during the Wakes service on Sunday last. I was intrigued concerning the practice of there being 'dog whippers'. Catherine told me that, in these parts, it was not uncommon for parishioners to bring their dogs along to Divine Worship. This practice was tolerated, but certainly not encouraged. It did, however, mean that on occasions stray dogs would wander into the church and it was for this reason that 'dog whippers' were employed, in order to ensure that only dogs which were accompanied by a parishioner were given access. It was the churchwardens at Eyam who acted in the capacity of 'dog whippers'. This was just another local custom which I found quite bizarre.

CHAPTER THREE
PLAGUE

Extract from the Journal of the Revd William Mompesson:
Wednesday 6 September 1665

I visited the home of Mrs Mary Hatfield earlier today. I had been informed
that her lodger, a certain Mr George Viccars, had died of a fever.

Although still somewhat distressed about the tragedy, especially in light
of the fact that her husband, Alexander, was away from the family home
on business at the time, Mrs Hatfield was able to acquaint me with the
details of this most unfortunate event. After collecting her thoughts she
told me that George Viccars, a journeyman tailor, was employed by her
husband as his assistant. Although Viccars was married he often worked
away from home, especially when there was an abundance of work, as
there currently was in the village because of the Wakes Festival. For the
duration of his employ, Viccars was staying at the Hatfield family home.

A box containing materials had been delivered earlier in the week. Mrs
Hatfield had no knowledge as to whether it was her husband who had
made the order or her lodger, but she did know that the box of material
had been sent from London. Mrs Hatfield went on to state that when
Viccars opened the box he found that, possibly because of the journey
from London, much of the material was damp and musty. He laid out the
material and dried it in front of the fire, as requested. But then, shortly
afterwards, he was violently sick; an event which troubled her children
greatly. The following day he became delirious, as huge swellings began to
manifest themselves on his neck and the area around his groin. Finally, on
the third day of his illness, the plague spot became evident upon his breast.
His agony continued until today, when he died.

I made arrangements to bury him on the morrow.

From the hand of Beth Hounsfeild:
Tuesday 12 September 1665

Earlier in the day, Catherine suggested that we should take advantage of the summer before the evening shadows lengthened. Walking from the rectory towards the western end of the churchyard, we passed the Coopers' dwelling where George Viccars had been a lodger. I'd heard that he was only a temporary resident in the village; Catherine thought that he had worked as a journeyman tailor and was employed by the new master of the home, Alexander Hadfield.

Apparently Mary Cooper, as she had been known until her recent marriage, was the widow of a lead miner to whom she had two sons, Jonathan and Edward. It seems that Edward Cooper, Mary's late husband, purchased the dwelling in 1662, but that he died shortly afterwards in 1664. In the terms of his will, he left the property to his two young sons, but made provision such that his widow retained a life interest. Rumour has it that the said Edward Cooper was a relatively wealthy man, the inventory of his effects were recorded as being in excess of £90. Also, according to William's understanding, he was owed somewhat more than £40 in outstanding debts and his inventory also makes reference to a plot of land, which he had recently purchased. Edward Cooper was obviously a literate man, being the owner of several books, including a copy of the Bible. The executor of his will was his beloved and trusty friend Thomas Wright of Unthank, a hamlet on the southern slopes of the Cordwell Valley not very far from Sheffield.

Catherine told me that in March of this year Mary remarried a travelling tailor, Mr Alexander Hatfield. He'd been called away on business some time in the last few weeks, so that, when a box of material was delivered to the family home, it was natural that George Viccars was instructed to open it. The box contained several bolts of cloth and also some material remnants, including camaca, a quantity of scrim, a bolt of balzarine and a small quantity of foulé which, I'm informed, is a light woollen fulled cloth. Catherine thought that much of the material in the box was of good quality, having been woven in Canterbury, but had been bought cheaply by a relative of either George Viccars or Alexander Hatfield, as it had come from plague-ridden London. It had even been suggested that there were some items of second-hand clothing amongst the various bolts of cloth, which, being London-made, were destined to be refashioned as new Derbyshire patterns.

But, when Viccars opened the box as instructed, he found much of the material to be moist – no doubt after its long and hazardous journey from London. It was clear that the cloth couldn't be worked upon in such a condition, so it was draped in front of the cottage-fire in order that it would dry out a little quicker than if left to dry naturally. It was just a short time after this that he was taken by a violet sickness, being delirious and running a fever. He died last Tuesday and William buried him on Wednesday. Catherine said that William had visited the household on the day that Viccars died and that, even though he was only a paid worker, Mrs Hadfield was very upset, especially at the terrible way in which he met his death.

William couldn't, or perhaps wouldn't, confirm it, but he was of the opinion that Viccars had died from the plague.

From the hand of Beth Hounsfeild:
Monday 18 September 1665

The death of George Viccars came as a terrible shock last week, although I believe that the circumstances surrounding it are not, as yet, widely known within the parish. But, as Catherine says, it's a very small village and news travels fast, especially when the circumstances surrounding the painful death were so unusual; the rumour mill will, doubtless, already be at work.

As we only have a couple of weeks left to spend in this delightful part of the country, Catherine thought that we might walk as far as the hamlet of Bretton today. The hamlet forms part of the parish and lies to the north-west of the village. William had parochial duties to attend to at the Town Head area of the parish so he walked with us that far, before we continued on our way following the road to Foolow. Although Catherine has oft talked of Bretton and Foolow – like Bretton, Foolow also lies within the bounds of William's parish – I've not had the opportunity to visit either of them, until today that is. When we were some way out of the village, we came to the farm at Shepherd's Flatt. Catherine said that the Kempe family and several different branches of the Morten family live in and around this area. Before leaving Shepherd's Flatt we met Luke and Joan Morten with their eleven-month-old baby, Mary. We stayed talking to them for some while. It was then but a short walk to the hamlet of Foolow, where we sat on the village green near to the pond. We then made our way towards Bretton itself. As we started to climb a light breeze was blowing across the moor and we could sense that all of the visiting swifts and swallows were now preparing to depart for another year. The summer flowers were also coming to an end, but the hedgerows still looked colourful with hawkweed, bindweed and the last of the cranesbill.

I was certainly in need of some respite when we arrived at the tiny hilltop hamlet sometime later; however, the views overlooking the moors and the valley more than compensated for our morning's effort. We sat for little while just outside of the hamlet, and were rewarded with more breathtaking views of Shepherd's Flatt and Foolow some way below us. We then continued on our way along the ridge top, and to the crest of the road. As the weather was still fine, rather than taking the footpath directly down back to the village, we decided to walk along the well-worn track to Highcliffe. Obviously the walk was much further than we'd originally anticipated, but it seemed too good a day to waste and there was no urgency to return to the rectory. We continued along the track known as the Edge, which lead us into Hawks Hill and then back into the village. It had been a good day's walk; Catherine thought that perhaps we'd walked upwards of six or seven miles.

Extract from the Journal of the Revd William Mompesson:
Wednesday 4 October 1665

The pestilence, having claimed the life of George Viccars, has now gained strength in our parish. There have been a further nine fatalities since Viccars death, the first, at the same property, being that of young Edward Cooper who was buried on 22 September, just one year after his father, Edward. The following day Peter Hawksworth, who lived next door to the Cooper family, died.

Earlier this morning I visited their neighbour William Thorpe, whose wife, Mary, died yesterday. Because of the worsening situation, he has seen fit to make provision for the dispersal of his goods and chattels in the event of his life being taken by the disease. Entrusted to my care is a copy of his last will and testament, which I have appended to this journal.

Before Mary died, their son Thomas, who lived nearby, was taken by the plague and was buried on 26 September. And then, just four days later, on 30 September, Thomas's eleven-year-old daughter, Mary, also fell victim and died, and then on Sunday last, his wife Elizabeth died.

In the name of God Amen. I William Thorpe of Eyam in the County of Darby yeoman beinge in good health and perfect memory blessed be god, but seeing by dayly experience the uncertainty of this transitory life by the hand of god upon my family Do make constitute ordaine and declare this my last will and Testament in manner and forme following. Revokinge and anullinge (by these presents) all and every Testament and Testaments, will and wills heretofore by me made and declared, eyther by word or writinge, and this to be taken onely for my last will and Testament and none other.

I committe my soule unto Almighty God, being fully assured, through his mercy, by the merits of Jesus Christ my Saviour and Redeemer to be saved eternally: and my body to the earth, to be buried at the discretion of my Executor hereafter named. And concerning my worldly estate my will and minde is as followeth.

All my goods and Chattels, moveable and unmoveable whatsoever, I give and bequeath (my debts and funerall first payed and discharged) unto Thomas Thorpe and Alice Thorpe, or the survivor of them, being son and daughter of my son Thomas Thorpe late deceased, for and towards theire bringinge up and education.

I give and bequeath unto Alice Thorpe my grandechilde aforesayd, fifteene pounds, to be payed out of my lands, when she shall accomplish the age of one and twenty years.

All my housinge and lands, I give and bequeath unto William Thorpe and Thomas Thorpe aforesayd or the survivor of them and to their heyrs, lawfully to be begotten. And for want of such issue my will and minde is That my said lands and housings returns to Robert Thorpe, eldest son of my sayd son Thomas Thorpe and to the heyrs of his Body lawfully to be begotten. And for want of such issue to Alice Thorpe aforesayd and to her heyrs lawfully to be begotten. And for want of such issue, my will and minde is, and I doe hereby declare it to be my Reall will and minde, that the said lands and housing goe, remaine, and be to and for she only use and behoofe of Abraham Broadhurst my wellbeloved cousin, son of George Broadhurst of Upper Haddon, and to his heyrs and assigns for ever.

Lastly I give and bequeath unto Robert Thorpe and William Thorpe aforesayd, eyther of them twenty shillings to be payd in one whole yeare after my descease. And I doe nominate and appoint John Wilson of Church-Style and the sayd Abraham Broadhurst Guardians to the sayd Alice Thorpe and Thomas Thorpe: and Executir of this my last will and Testament desiring them to take this charge upon them not doubting but they will execute it according to the true intent and meanings thereof. In witness whereof I have hereunto putt my hand and scale The third day of October 1665.

William Thorpe

In the presence of us

John Hancock
John Chapman his marke
Anthony Raworth

Sarah Syddall, a near neighbour living on the far side of the road, was struck dead from the disease on Saturday last. Matthew Banes died on Sunday 1 October, followed by his wife, Margaret, who died yesterday. I visited the household earlier this morning. Mary Banes, Matthew's widowed mother said that she would take care of Martha Banes, Matthew's two-year old daughter, and also his nine-month-old baby, Mary.

I pray every day that this pestilence may soon cease.

Extract from the Journal of the Revd William Mompesson:
Sunday 8 October 1665

After taking a copy of the last will and testament of William Thorpe, which he made on Tuesday last, 3 October 1665, I had occasion to re-read it this morning, following the office of Divine Worship. I received information which confirmed that he, like his dear wife Mary, has now succumbed to this terrible plague. I am now therefore faced with the duty of informing John Wilson of Church-Style and Abraham Broadhurst, William's cousin, of their roles and responsibilities as guardians to his grandchildren, Alice Thorpe and Thomas Thorpe.

Having now read through the will once again, no mention as to guardianship is made relating to either Thomas's youngest son, four-year-old William, or his sixteen-year-old son, Robert – both of their parents, Thomas Thorpe and Elizabeth Thorpe, having died in the last two weeks. I can only assume that, in the case of young William, that this is an oversight, and that, perhaps William considered that Robert, now reaching manhood, could therefore look after himself. I will approach John Wilson and Abraham Broadhurst in relation to both of these matters.

From the hand of Beth Hounsfeild:
Monday 16 October 1665

The pallid sun rested low in the clear October sky this morning, yet somehow seemed to kindle a ray of hope into our weary hearts. So far, seventeen souls have been consumed by the plague which has beset the village. After breakfast Catherine and I walked over to the thatched cottage of the Syddall family, witnessing as we went a squall in the gentle breeze sending myriads of leaves quietly tumbling down, weaving their autumnal carpet on the ground around us. On our way, she told me of the tragedies that had befallen that family over the last two months. Living more or less directly across the road from the lodgings of George Viccars, the plague had visited them very early. Young Sarah Syddall, the plague's fifth victim, had succumbed on the very last day of September and then earlier this month Richard, her seven-year-old brother, was the next victim in that household. The children's father, John Syddall, died of the plague two days ago. As three of the family's other daughters, Ellen, Elizabeth and Alice, are now showing plague symptoms, Emmott – with whom Catherine has had many meetings during the last few weeks – has asked for some plague remedies; their household store having been completely exhausted on other members of the family.

When we arrived we learnt that Ellen had died and been buried yesterday, and that Elizabeth and Alice were now in the final throes of the plague.

On our way back to the rectory, Catherine told me of Emmott's betrothal to Rowland Torre of Stoney Middleton. They are due to be married at Wakeside but realistically, if the pestilence continues as it is, she feels that the Wakes next year will be very different from those we enjoyed earlier this year.

William and the Revd Stanley arrived back at the rectory some minutes after our return. They informed us that Martha Banes, Jonathan Ragge and Humphrey Hawkesworth, Peter's baby son, have all fallen ill. The pestilence seems to be progressing from one family to another.

From the Diary of Catherine Mompesson:
Saturday 21 October 1665

Following the visit of the Revd Stanley directly after breakfast this morning, William informed me that young Martha Banes had died on Tuesday last and that her grandmother, Mary Banes – who was caring for both her and her baby sister following the deaths of both of their parents – had also died early yesterday afternoon. William asked me to visit and try to make some arrangements for the care of the one remaining member of the family, the nine-month-old baby, Mary Banes.

Extract from the Journal of the Revd William Mompesson:
Saturday 4 November 1665

This morning I visited the Rowlands' dwelling where, I fear, Hannah may not be far from death, she too now having succumbed to this awful pestilence. Already this month there have been two further deaths, that of Hugh Stubbs and baby Alice Taylor. October is a month that I'm relieved has now passed as twenty-three parishioners died from the pestilence, including members from the Thorpe family, the Torres, the Banes, the Syddalls and the Ragges. Also, Humphrey Hawksworth was buried on the 17th of the month. The situation is now becoming desperate and I own to being at a loss as to what actions to take, in order to alleviate the suffering and mitigate the effects of this terrible plague which has befallen us. I have however been comforted by the support given to me by a former incumbent of the parish, the Nonconformist pastor, the Revd Thomas Stanley. Again, I must own to having some reservations as to this support, because of his fervently held puritanical views. However, because of the many divergences of opinion within the parish, some people are still harbouring Nonconformist allegiances and also pay allegiance to the man himself. It is for this reason that I am loath to accept his support, but recognise the political value in demonstrating a united front to the parishioners against the pestilence. On the one hand, his presence in the village is invaluable, since he manifests such a calming influence on a significant number of the parishioners who still hold, however covertly, this allegiance to Puritan doctrines. However, the counterargument – one which I must, in my position, never fail to take into consideration – is the fact that he is living in direct contravention to the Act of Conformity and also the recently enacted Five Mile Act.

After dinner this evening I discussed the issue with Edward. We retired to my study where I expanded upon some of my innermost thoughts with regards to the situation. Edward was aware of the ramifications relating to the Act of Uniformity, especially the declaration of 'unfeigned assent and consent' to everything contained in the Book of Common Prayer, and the re-ordination for those not episcopally ordained. We also discussed the stipulation 'that all ministers in the Church of England must conform to the demands of this Act by St Bartholomew's Day, 24 August, 1662'. I disclosed to Edward the fact that I was aware that the Revd Stanley had, upon this date, chosen to publicly declare his true allegiances, by his renunciation of the Act, and that this lay heavily on my conscience. I had many misgivings in relationship to this Act and also the Revd Stanley's stance here. Edward and I then discussed the more recent Five Mile Act, with which he was less familiar. I informed him that it forbade clergymen from living within five miles of a parish from which they had been expelled, unless they swore an oath never to resist the King or attempt to alter the government of Church or State, and I was aware that the Revd Stanley had not sworn this oath. Further, I knew that the swearing of this oath was anathema to Stanley and, as I said to Edward, it left me in an invidious position with regards to how that may affect my decision as to whether or not to accept Stanley's offer of support.

Before retiring, I prayed fervently for guidance, as I must seek some resolution this deplorable state of affairs. One positive thing, which did emerge from our conversation, was that I would seek to engage Stanley in discussion in the near future.

From the Diary of Catherine Mompesson:
Sunday 26 November 1665

We saw the first light covering of snow this morning. During our service of Divine Worship, I had heard that Elizabeth Warrington was unwell. After lunch, I walked to the house which she had jointly inherited with her sister, Mary Rowe, from their mother.

Leaving the rectory, there was a light carpet of white, twinkling with hoar frost which, even at this late hour, was still in evidence. I had taken a plague remedy which I'd obtained from Humphrey Merrill. He told me that Mary Rowland and Richard Coyle were also in need of medicaments, as they too were now showing the first signs of having succumbed to the distemper.

From the Diary of Catherine Mompesson:
Tuesday 6 February 1666

It was shortly after Beth and Edward arrived that I'd walked out with her to the tiny hamlet of Bretton, which lies towards the outer edge of the parish. We'd walked via Shepherd's Flatt, where many of the Morten families live, before venturing on to the hamlet itself. So, it was with some foreboding that I received the news that William reported at dinner this evening. During the morning he'd met a parishioner in the village who had just come from the hamlet – a journey of less than two miles. She'd told him that the pestilence has now reached there and that, so far, there are a number of souls who are beginning to show signs of having fallen victim to the distemper. William was not aware of their names, but had been told that already one of the older householders, who is recorded on the Foolow Returns as Peter Morten, had died on Sunday last. In addition to Peter Morten's family, there are the families of Michael, Matthew, Isaac, Francis and Luke Morten. I asked if there were any remedies required, but William said that he would be visiting the village with the Revd Stanley on the morrow, so he would let me know on his return.

Extract from the Journal of the Revd William Mompesson:
Wednesday 7 February 1666

I walked over to Shepherd's Flatt with the Revd Stanley, my brother-in-Christ, this morning. We stopped first at the home of the late Peter Morten and found his wife, Joan, and his two children, Elizabeth and Michael, in good health. We enquired about other Morten families, only to be told that they too were in rude health – comforting news. It would appear that Peter Morten's death might be an isolated occurrence. Since the back-end of last year, there have been few deaths: Praise God.

From the Diary of Catherine Mompesson:
Sunday 25 February 1666

After leaving church this morning following Divine Worship, I heard that Mrs Elizabeth Abell had given birth to her first child, a daughter who was to be baptised with the name of Mary. It's the first good news that we've heard in the parish for many weeks now, as most conversation inevitably centres on the continuing presence of the pestilence which, it has to be said, has become a little less aggressive during these last winter months. I pray fervently to the Almighty that this curse may soon be lifted from our village.

It was a chill wind that blew through the village as Beth and I set out for the Abell homestead sometime after lunch. We left William and Edward to await the arrival of the Revd Stanley, following his round of visiting to the sick and needy of the parish; a task which he cheerfully fulfils on a daily basis during these testing times which we all have to endure.

Beth first met Mrs Abell when she visited the rectory, shortly after her marriage. I remember it well, she came to tell us more about some of the ancient traditions which are still practised in and around the parish. Both Beth and myself have made her acquaintance on many subsequent occasions but none, I dare to say, were to be as significant as our meeting today. We were met at the door by Mr Abell who faced us with a look of utter despair, incredulity and resignation. Instinctively, both Beth and I were immediately of the same mind, that Mrs Abell had been visited by the plague. Upon entering the house, we were to find that this was not the case, but that during childbirth, she had suffered greatly, due to the absence of any women from the parish who could assist at the birth. The baby was in a crib next to the lying-in bed, but Mrs Abell hardly responded to our presence and greetings.

Little was said between Beth and myself on our return to the rectory; both knowing that nothing short of a miracle is now needed.

Extract from the Journal of the Revd William Mompesson:
Wednesday 28 February 1666

Following the visit of my dear wife, Catherine, to the bed of Mrs Elizabeth Abell on Sunday last, I was informed this morning that the dear lady had since passed away. I made it my business to visit Christopher Abell. His mind was deeply disturbed when I called – having to bury his wife after less than two years of marriage, and now being faced with the nurture and upbringing a young suckling baby. It is possible that there might be a woman who could act as a wet nurse for the baby, but that is problematical given the current dire situation in the village. I said that I would make inquiries, but, in truth, I fear that alternative arrangements of some sort will have to be arranged.

From the Diary of Catherine Mompesson:
Friday 20 April 1666

A pot of coarse plum conserve had been brought to the rectory yesterday by one of the miners' wives, so we enjoyed that at breakfast. Although it left a slightly bitter aftertaste, it nonetheless much enhanced the frugal fayre of oat cakes and bread that we've been enduring for some considerable time now.

After the remains of breakfast had been sided away, I suggested to Beth that she might wish to accompany me on my round of ministrations this morning. From conversations which William had related, I was aware that Elizabeth Hadfield's fifteen-year-old son, Samuel, had been taken by the pestilence on Wednesday, and this coming less than eighteen months since her dear husband, Hugh, had died. This was our first visit.

Leaving the putrid smells of death and disease which were still present in the cottage, we next hastened towards the home of the Thorpe family whose grief was unbounded, having already lost their father, Thomas, mother, Elizabeth, and siblings, Mary and Thomas, towards the latter end of last year. And now on Sunday, their one remaining sister, Alice, had been claimed by the pestilence. Robert, just sixteen years of age, was left to look after and care for his four-year-old brother, William. However, on our path to their cottage we encountered Margaret Blackwell's elder brother, Francis. From my limited knowledge of him, I had always found him to be a somewhat reserved, even dour, individual who rarely indulged in idle gossip or tittle-tattle and, on the few occasions that he did engage in conversation, it was generally because of dire necessity. This morning, however, he appeared to be positively encumbered with the deepest of emotions. He was thirteen years older than Margaret, whom I had made the acquaintance of on a fairly regular basis. Their young brother, Anthony, had died on Christmas Eve last year, and then their father had been taken by the plague late in February. Since that time, their two sisters, Ann and Joan, had died and just four days ago their mother, Margaret, had also died; leaving only Francis and his sister, Margaret, to look after one another. His manner was much milder this morning, even ingratiating, but carried a degree of urgency; yet he still managed to maintain a balanced temperament. His visage, normally cold and somewhat aloof – as though he had a marked indifference to most of the events happening around him – was very different this morning.

He addressed me directly: 'Mistress Mompesson, it is indeed fortuitous that we should meet as, even now, I must leave my dear infirmed sister in order to obtain coal from the pit. My journey necessitates my absence for a goodly part of the day, and, on my return, I fear for her well-being. She is, I believe, in the final throes of the plague.'

'Mister Blackwell, we will indeed visit your dear sister, but first we have urgent business at the home of the Thorpe family.'

Without more ado we continued on our journey, as did Mr Blackwell. As promised, on our return from the Thorpes' we called at the Blackwell residence in Rock Square, unsure as to what scene would await us. To our complete surprise and relief, we were greeted by Margaret herself, who, although not being a picture of health, was certainly in a different condition from the way her brother had described her some two or three hours earlier. She related the events of the day to us:

My brother, having to leave the home early for his long journey to the pit, cooked some bacon for his breakfast before he left. Normally I would have cooked, but, having blurred vision and being in a state of delirium, I was unable to rise from my bed. After Francis's departure, the fever must have reached its height, as an insatiable and maddening thirst was brought upon me. I managed to leave my bed and made my way to the kitchen where, seizing the nearest vessel that I could find, a wooden piggin, I drank ardently from it. I thought that it was boiled milk, but, some while later, realised that it was indeed the liquid fat from my brother's breakfast bacon. It's difficult to recall what happened next, but I think that I must have vomited at some point afterwards, and then I slept for most of the remainder of the morning. I have been drifting between consciousness and unconsciousness, not knowing whether I was dreaming or not, but now, upon hearing your knock, I feel so much better.

We left Margaret Blackwell waiting for her brother to return from the pit; he would doubtless be more than surprised to witness Margaret's miraculous recovery.

Extract from the Journal of the Revd William Mompesson:
Thursday 26 April 1666

After a long day's toil about the parish with my brother-in-Christ, the Revd Stanley, I suggested to Edward that before dinner I would shew him two of the inns in the village, both of which had a particular significance in the parish. Although not venturing in, I first took him to see the Kings Head in Water Lane, where many of the miners used to meet after a day's work. I related that the tavern, having been burned down in 1629, was subsequently rebuilt in 1630, some thirty-five years before the visitation of the plague. When the original tavern was burned down, two young girls, Emily and Sarah, tragically lost their lives. Many people who frequent the tavern have suggested that they can hear light footsteps, skipping from one room to another. It has even been intimated that I should go and exorcise the place, but I haven't been approached by the owner as yet. I know that some residents have complained about their slumbers being disturbed due to various ghostly activities, including chamber doors being opened and closed at regular intervals, only to be immediately followed by peals of laughing and giggling emanating from the adjacent corridors.

I then took him along to our other tavern in the village, the Royal Oak. This inn, built in 1587, was originally called the Heart of Oak; a reference to British seamen. The inn was completely rebuilt in 1660 and renamed the Royal Oak – in homage to the restoration of the monarchy.

From the Diary of Catherine Mompesson:
Monday 30 April 1666

After losing her husband, John, and most of her children in October of last year, the widow, Elizabeth Syddall, married widower John Daniel on Tuesday last, 24 April.

I went to visit the family this morning, knowing that since the wedding, Emmott, Elizabeth's betrothed daughter, was showing signs of having caught the plague. I'd taken a remedy with me but as soon as I entered the home I realised, from the putrid odour assailing my nostrils, that Emmott had indeed passed away. She had died and had been buried in the field next to the house yesterday. Elizabeth was grief-stricken and Joseph, not yet three year old, was bereft, having lost his only sister.

Elizabeth talked of Emmott's meetings with her betrothed, Rowland Torre. Knowing of the risk of passing infection to the neighbouring village of Stoney Middleton, where Rowland's father was a flour-miller, she had implored them not to continue meeting. But he, wishing to console Emmott in her time of need, had continued to make his daily journey over to the village. Then, as the pestilence took a firmer stranglehold, his visits did cease but Elizabeth believed that they had continued to have secret meetings in the Delph, where at least they'd have been able to see one another from a distance and know that all was well. It was Elizabeth's belief that Rowland had not been told of the death of his beloved Emmott, although she thought that he must have had some inkling of her illness.

Extract from the Journal of the Revd William Mompesson:
Thursday 3 May 1666

Both Robert Thorpe and his younger brother, William, died yesterday. This means that, since September last year, all of Thomas Thorpe's family, including himself and also his wife, Elizabeth, have died. And although their relatives, Robert and Margaret Thorpe, are still living in the village, their children, Thomas, Elizabeth, Robert and Richard, have all died as a result of this terrible plague which has befallen our tiny parish.

From the Diary of Catherine Mompesson:
Friday 11 May 1666

It had been some weeks since I had seen Margaret Blackwell in the village; indeed, I believe that it was the day when Beth and I met her brother when he was on his way to the pit. By now she had made a complete recovery and attributed this to the timely administration of her unconventional prophylactic! She went on to recount how utterly surprised and perplexed her brother had been on his return from the pit. I intimated that William thought that the pestilence might be abating, as there had only been five deaths in the village since her miraculous recovery. I did however disclose that I was journeying to the home of James Taylor, who, I believed, was in the last throes of the plague. Before leaving her, we talked of the omen which I witnessed last year at Divine Worship. At the Wake, a number of youths had driven a young cow into the church. Fortunately, the 'dog whippers' managed to remove the terrified animal from the church. I knew that it was a portent of something, but at the time I did not know what. Margaret then told a story which related to events which occurred at Padley Hall, some short distance from Eyam, towards the end of the last century. The hall, which at that time was becoming a centre of Catholic influence in the High Peak, was owned by Sir Thomas Fitzherbert and rented to his brother, John Fitzherbert, a known Catholic recusant. In July 1588, it was raided by agents of the Earl of Shrewsbury, with the express purpose of arresting the said John Fitzherbert. Upon entering, the agents found two Jesuit priests offering Mass. Both were local men, Robert Ludlam from Whirlow, near to Sheffield, and Nicholas Garlick, of Glossop – he was formerly a schoolmaster in Tideswell. They were arrested and taken to Derby for trial. On their journey they passed through Eyam and villagers, knowing of their misdemeanour, reviled them. The priests were then heard to utter curses on the village and its people and this, said Margaret, was an omen of disaster and a prediction of the plague. Not knowing of the tale, I asked her what the ultimate fate of the priests was. She looked at me aghast and told me that they were tried on 23 July 1588 and found guilty of treason. They were hung, drawn and quartered the next day at St Mary's Bridge, in Derby. I left Margaret, not knowing if my questioning had offended her.

When I arrived at the home of James Taylor, I was met by his kinsfolk, Thomas and Mary Taylor, who told me that James, who lived on his own, had died some hours ago – but not, according to them, from the plague. I did not tarry for too long, as Thomas and Mary Taylor together with Sarah Taylor, had, only last year, been excommunicated for fornication.

William was sorry to hear of James Taylor's death, but was not overly pleased with me for having spent time with his disgraced kinsfolk.

Extract from the Journal of the Revd William Mompesson:
Thursday 17 May 1666

Following the deaths of Robert and William Thorpe earlier this month, there has only been one recorded death, that of James Taylor on 11 May. As Catherine went to visit him on the actual day of his death, she indicated to me that, with her wealth of knowledge relating to plague symptoms, she had reason to believe that his death might not have been caused as a direct result of the plague. However, as I did not see the corpse before committal, I cannot be sure. But, there are other happenings, which lead me to believe that this terrible curse may be coming to an end. My esteemed colleague, the Revd John Walker from the Parish of Hathersage, has communicated to me that the pestilence in London appears to be in decline; I pray God that this may be so.

After prayer this morning, I discussed my continuing concerns with the Revd Stanley. At the termination of our conversation we agreed that, provided there were no more plague deaths before the end of the month, or at least one and twenty days from the date of the deaths of Robert and William Thorpe, then perhaps we might not need to consider any restrictive measures for the people of the parish.

CHAPTER FOUR
DECISIONS ARE TAKEN

From the Diary of Catherine Mompesson:
Monday 18 June 1666

Beth and I spent a goodly part of the morning visiting a number of homes in the parish whose families were in need of remedies against the fatal malady which is now plumbing hitherto unfathomable depths. First we visited the Thornley household where Isaac died at the beginning of the month. Since that time Anna, Jonathan, Elizabeth and Francis have all died, and now we have been told that Jane too is stricken with early symptoms of the plague. We arrived too late; Jane had been buried at dawn this morning, having died in the early hours. Leaving there, we made our way to the Skidmore home, where ten-year-old Anthony died less than a week ago and his elder sister, Mary, was buried just yesterday. We have been told that widow Anne Skidmore is in desperate need of a remedy, as she is now in a state of delirium as a result of the plague. We had intended visiting the Mowers', as we'd been told that both James and his six-year-old sister Edytha had died, but lack of time precluded our visit.

When winter was upon us, we thought that we might have seen the end of the visitation, but, alas, that wasn't to be. In March we had seen fifty-six dear souls from the parish laid to their eternal rest, and then in April there were, mercifully, just nine deaths. In May only three deaths were recorded. I recall that William had prayed fervently that this signalled the end of our ordeal, but maybe it isn't to be, as now, deaths from the plague are becoming an everyday occurrence and there's every indication that matters are getting worse by the hour – since the start of the month, there have been twelve more deaths. People in the village are filled with fear, wondering where the plague will strike next. I have spent many long hours agonising at the courageous decision which Beth and Edward took some time ago to remain with us in the parish, but I am increasingly beginning to question its wisdom; and also that of William and me for agreeing to sanction such a noble decision. Whenever I look at Beth's crestfallen countenance, she always seems to be deep in thought. I sometimes wonder if her thoughts run along similar lines to mine. Although no mention had been made of the decision since it had been taken, I felt that, in fairness to her and Edward, we needed to reconsider the decision. As we walked along the now deserted lanes before reaching the rectory, I asked her if, in light of all the horrendous events which had occurred in the parish since the decision had been taken, she still considered it to be correct. Her response both shocked and reassured me. It was Beth's considered opinion that all of us, not just her and Edward, should quit the parish and return at a later date. She cited cases of clergy in other parishes up and down the country who, when faced with a similar situation to ours, had moved (albeit on a temporary basis) to adjoining parishes, returning when the pestilence had departed. I too had heard rumours that other families had recently moved out of the village and I knew that the Bradshaws had left for, I believe, Treeton. She implored me for everyone's sake, not least the children's, to plead with William to depart the parish. I said that William had already contacted relatives in the county of York to look after the children, should the need arise, but we hadn't contemplated any other, more drastic, measures. I did pledge that I would try to discuss the matter with William when he returned to the rectory, but cautioned that I couldn't be sure of his reaction.

William was late coming home this evening, as he too had spent some time over at the Thornleys' home, consoling Elizabeth Thornley. Elizabeth, a widow, had remarried in February 1664 and the marriage had been blessed with a young son, Francis. He had been buried yesterday and Elizabeth was, understandably, distraught. William's parochial duties are now weighing more heavily on his shoulders, even with the continuing and unfailing support of the Revd Stanley; and I know also from his continuous self-questioning, that the burthen of care towards his family exercises his thoughts constantly. My own state of helplessness has grown in magnitude throughout the past weeks, especially during this current week, culminating with the sentiments which Beth expressed earlier in the day and which, I have to own, reflect and echo my own feelings. Thus, before the children were taken to bed, I took them into William's study and cast them and myself at his feet, imploring him to take us to a place of safety away from the village. William, after agonising for some many minutes, bent down and gently raised myself and the children to his breast. In tender words, and with tears streaming, unquenched, down his sorrowful face, he told us that his duty lay here, to tend to the needs of his diminishing flock. His conscience would not allow him to desert them, in this, their greatest hour of need. I was aware that William had some misgivings about the parish when we first arrived, but whether it was because of the smallness of the living or the singular lack of society, I cannot tell. Be that as it may, he was determined that, because of his earlier misgivings and discontentment, he would now remain with his parishioners. His prayer, oft repeated, being 'God grant that I may repent my sad ingratitude'.

Extract from the Journal of the Revd William Mompesson:
Tuesday 19 June 1666

My visit to Elizabeth Thornley yesterday had taken considerably more time than I had envisioned. Her son, Francis, by this her second marriage, had died on Sunday before reaching his second birthday. She was overcome with grief. Upon my return I retired to my study for further contemplation and prayer. Some minutes later, my dear wife, accompanied by George and Elizabeth entered and prostrated themselves before me. She remained kneeling for some time, as did the children, and implored me to leave the parish and take them to a place of safety – stating that, because of the increasing virulence of the plague, the burthen was too much for them to bear any longer. I had no answer and prayed fervently to God for guidance. Summoning all that remained of my expended energy and powers, I raised Catherine and our dear children to my breast and held them tightly; firm in the knowledge that we would be given comfort and succour from our Lord and Redeemer. I could do little more than affirm my faith and, with faltering heart and words, told them that it was my God-given duty to remain true to my flock and to God's calling and, charged with this awful responsibility, the task was now more important than life itself.

When the children had departed and been taken to bed, I reaffirmed that arrangements were in hand to take her and our dear children to my uncle, Mr John Beilby, in the county of York. But my still tearful wife would not countenance such a parting, categorically stating that her duty was to remain here with me. I gave God thanks for her unfailing fortitude. We did, however, agree that it was perhaps in the children's best interests that they should be at some distance from the parish at this time. It was a difficult decision to reach but we agreed that, however detrimental it may be for ourselves, it was better for the children's well-being.

From the Diary of Catherine Mompesson:
Tuesday 19 June 1666

It was still dark outside when I awoke, earlier than usual, this morning. A wind had blown up during the night and I could see the shadows of the trees swaying, as the incessant rain beat upon the windowpanes. I knew that William was leaving the rectory early this morning and I wished to talk with him about some of my concerns, which had been left unresolved last night. Since the first deaths from the plague William's normally placid temperament had been much troubled, lurching between despondency on the one hand, to an almost evangelical zeal on the other, when mindful of the task which lay ahead. Amongst many other matters, we'd discussed the continuing exodus of several families from in and around the village, including the Bradshaws and the Sheldons who had left several months ago. I knew that this placed a heavy burthen upon William's shoulders, as these departures increased the risk of the pestilence spreading to our near neighbours. William had made reference last night to some of the measures already being taken. At Sheffield, he said that people from our parish couldn't gain access, the constables accounts had recorded: 'Charges about keeping people from Fullwood Spaw in the tyme that the sickness was att Eam.' 'For watching one that fell sick.' Considering the plight of the villagers, having insufficient crops and diary produce to be self-sufficient (being a predominantly lead mining village), William said that these considerations needed to be taken into account, and that, somehow, supplies of basic essentials and medicaments needed to be maintained if the village was to survive. It was already becoming more and more difficult to obtain fuel; people visiting the coal pits were forced to take unnecessarily long circuitous routes, in order to give the impression that they were coming from places other than Eyam. William had heard of one man who had, inadvertently, stated that he came from the parish. He suffered greatly and was forced to return home without any fuel. Whatever else was preying upon his mind at this time, the need to keep supplies coming into the village was clearly exercising him.

Before leaving with the Revd Stanley, I voiced, yet again, my concerns about our family's welfare, but William would not countenance any further discussion on the subject.

From the Diary of Catherine Mompesson:
Wednesday 20 June 1666

Sleep could not comfort me last night, for I knew that today my dear hearts, George and Elizabeth, would be taken from the parish. We broke our fast early this morning, as they were being transported to our relative J. Bielby, Esq., over in Sheffield; where they would stay until the pestilence should cease.

Last night before retiring, William had begged me once again to accompany them today; suggesting that it would be much better if I was there to look after their well-being. But, much as I love my dear children and would dearly wish to be with them, my first duty is here with my husband.

Breaking with his normal practice, William himself brought the children into breakfast. On their way in, I heard him reminding George – who is almost four years old now – not only to look after his young sister while they are away, but also to be good and obedient. I detected an agonised tension in William's voice which is never normally present; I fear that he too is engulfed in doubt and misgivings. I just hope and pray that our dear babes won't be gone for too long; we will miss them so much.

All too soon I was holding them tight to my breast never wanting to let them go, but let them go I must. As they left the rectory, I felt that my heart would burst. I returned to William's study, where we offered prayers for their safe-keeping – not knowing when or if we would be seeing them again.

The Revd Stanley visited the rectory on his way to see Edward Thornley, who has now succumbed to the pestilence. William accompanied him, as there were urgent items of parochial business which he wanted to discuss.

My duty is to be by the side of my husband, but I own that without Beth's cheerful company, I would be totally bereft. Today has been a very dark day.

From the Diary of Catherine Mompesson:
Thursday 21 June 1666

Clearly deeply troubled from our fraught discussions on Monday last and the subsequent departure of the children, William abruptly curtailed his breakfast and went about his daily business somewhat earlier than was his accustomed hour. I surmised that, because of his grave countenance and uncharacteristic actions, he must be lost in thought; no doubt considering the enormity of the task still facing himself and his brother-in-Christ, the Revd Stanley. I reflected that almost since the earliest days of the visitation the usual offices which attended death, rituals such as recitation from the prayer book and the scattering of earth, had by common consent been dispensed with; this was by reason of mere practicality and expediency. Another time-honoured ceremony, of the strewing herbs and flowers prior to the funeral processions of spinsters of the parish, was also abandoned. Similarly, the carrying of funeral garlands before the cortège – subsequently to be hung from the church rafters as a symbol of their chastity – was also curtailed. All sentiment, grieving and due ceremony being suspended *pro tempore*.

Following death, family members would begin the gruesome task of burial. The family, and only the family, for no others would venture near to a body that was not a member of his, undertook this thankless task, carrying the corpse to the prepared grave on a makeshift bier or even in some cases being dragged on a length of cloth or towelling. But, as members of families become fewer in number, dire necessity has driven people to seek alternative means of ensuring that the corpse is speedily removed and buried with all haste. It was in this capacity that Marshall Howe, a lead miner living in the village, found his true, if unpalatable, vocation in life; he took upon himself the unenviable role of plague sexton and burier of the dead.

It was all too apparent as to why Howe had assumed the responsibility as, in the very first days of the plague, he himself had taken the distemper, but had subsequently made a full recovery. It used to be a currently held view that, having recovered, he was now immune from further attack. It was this belief that no doubt accounted, in part, for his total lack of respect for the disease, and irreverence towards those whom he buried.

From my infrequent dealings with Howe, I formed the opinion that he was a taciturn individual, not particularly given to communication of any meaningful length or import; but, unlike many of his fellow miners, his physique could only be described as being truly gigantic. He was very sturdily built. His face, apart from the obvious ravages brought about by many years of mining, was not unpleasant. His broad cheekbones, together with his deep-set dark eyes, conveyed to me an impression of him being resolute and determined in manner, but whether this was the case was somewhat difficult to ascertain.

It was rumoured that, as soon as he had been informed of an imminent death and there being no family member remaining to perform the task of interment, he would reconnoitre the area as to suitability and also assess the spoils likely to result from his endeavours. Then, more often than not with unseemly haste, he would open a grave in a nearby field, or the dead person's garden, before entering the house to secure a chord around the feet of the sometimes still warm corpse. He would then, without any further ceremony, drag the body to the prepared shallow grave. It was even stated that, on occasions, the rope had been secured around the dead person's neck if it was considered that this would result in a quicker disposal. Finally, before recovering the rewards of his labours, the grave was given a light and cursory covering of earth.

During the days when ale was still freely available from the village alehouse, Marshall Howe, holding court with a surly and smug expression, would tell of the compensation which he accorded himself, rifled from the homes of those he buried; boasting of the cache of furniture, money, clothes and other effects of the deceased, which he had accumulated as his unenviable remuneration. Giving an extensive inventory of his ill-gotten plunder, his oft-quoted claim was that he had 'pinners and napkins enough to kindle his pipe while he lived'.

Beth forwarded many theories as to the driving force behind Howe's hazardous vocation, but, without having the benefit of an understanding of the mind of a lead miner, speculation was rendered futile; my own simple belief was that it was, purely and simply, cupidity and an overwhelming desire to rid himself of the mine that enabled him to continue, and even relish, his ghoulish avocation.

Extract from the Journal of the Revd William Mompesson:
Thursday 21 June 1666

Throughout the day, as I visited several more needy homes, I had been pondering measures which might safeguard peoples' health and security or at least help in some way to alleviate their plight. Before retiring, I voiced some of my concerns to Catherine, but first we talked at some considerable length about our decision to send the children away. It had been an agonising decision for both of us but, in our hearts, we knew that it had been correct. When our discussion turned to the worsening situation in the parish, Catherine commented that since the end of May, when I may have, inadvertently, shown misplaced and unjustified optimism as to the demise of the pestilence, the number of deaths has now begun to rise again quite significantly. Even since the start of this month, five members of the Thornley family have died, as have two members of the Skidmore family, Anthony and Mary Skidmore. I've also been told that James Mower, Elizabeth Buxton, Mary Heald and Sarah Lowe have died; and today, I've been informed that both Mary Mellor and widow Anne Townend have both died since the beginning of the week.

It has been clear from the outset of this terrible infliction that families who were able to leave the village have done so; but most, because of their occupations in farming or working at the lead mines, have found that to be a course of action not available to them. Similarly, there is the fact that many of the families living in the village have spent most, if not all, of their lives in the immediate environs and have little or no knowledge of where kith and kin, who reside outside of Eyam, may have their habitation. Some children of parishioners have been sent to different relatives for the duration of the visitation, as indeed have our own dear children. I'm aware that the Sheldon and Furness families have moved from the village; the Sheldons to a property which they own in Hazleford, and the Furnesses have sought refuge at a farmhouse which I believe is about a mile distant from Eyam. I've also learned that some families have built makeshift accommodation near to Riley. Earlier in the year, much to my dismay, the widow of Squire George Bradshaw and her daughter, Ann, left Bradshaw Hall. I have to say the sad fact remains that there is nobody of stature left within the village, and the weight of leadership and decision-making falls squarely on my shoulders.

Before drawing our conversation to a close, Catherine went on to inform me that in recent weeks, access to Monday's market at Bakewell, just seven miles away, has been restricted. People who are known to be from the village are no longer allowed into the market town; if they need to purchase goods, they must, before receiving their purchases, place money in the stream that was formerly known as Stockingcote, which now, for some reason, is called Mondaybrook. In many respects perhaps this is an understandable departure, in that the good people of Bakewell need to safeguard their own interests. Catherine suggested that maybe I would be well advised to discuss the situation further with Beth's husband, Edward, because he, having had experience of such matters, may be able to shed some light on the wider significance and ramifications of any actions which I may propose.

Extract from the Journal of the Revd William Mompesson:
Friday 22 June 1666

Even since my conversation with Catherine on Wednesday evening, there have been further deaths in the village. I have been told that Abel Archdale died on Wednesday and Edward Thornley, whom I visited with the Revd Stanley on Wednesday morning, died earlier today. Naturally, I was extremely perplexed when I met with Edward, knowing that radical action now needs to be taken, but who is there to make these critical decisions and enforce the necessary actions? I pondered as to the role that the Revd Stanley is currently fulfilling; Edward too is also totally aware of the former Nonconformist rector's position within the parish. He acknowledged the fact that, on the one hand, there is a delicate balance to be preserved when placed in the context of the Act of Uniformity and the recent Five Mile Act, but, on the other hand, there is the undoubted allegiance and respect which the Revd Stanley still commands within the parish, to be taken into consideration. Edward is fully aware that I was only inducted into the parish in July 1664, following the death (in April of that year) of the Revd Shoreland Adams. I was therefore a relative newcomer and, it is clear from the villagers' appraisal of me, that I am not, as yet, regarded as being of the same calibre as the Revd Stanley. There is still a degree of reticence amongst some of the parishioners who do not wholeheartedly accept me as rector. This is undoubtedly due to the esteem in which the former Nonconformist rector was held and perhaps also, to some extent, the fact that I am still only twenty-eight years of age, whereas Stanley is many years my senior. I need not dwell on the fact that our living at Scalby was very different from our living here. I had thought that the Peak District would be a better environment for both my consumptive wife and my two young children, but I've been forced on occasions to question the wisdom of this decision.

Edward agreed that, viewing the situation from a dispassionate and non-partisan standpoint, it was self-evident that there were still serious problems in the village, having just come through, in the last three or four years, a very troubled time. The two previous rectors, the Revd's Shoreland Adams and Thomas Stanley, had served the parish for a total of some thirty-four years. Adams had been rector of the parish since 1630, but when the Nonconformist Puritans gained ascendency in 1644, Adams was removed and replaced by Thomas Stanley. Stanley served until 1660, when he was removed and Adams reappointed; this was totally due to the Act of Uniformity. I am lead to believe that, in actual fact, Stanley remained in the village and served in some clerical capacity, possibly that of Priest-in-Charge, due to the absence of Shoreland Adams (who tended to spend most of his time in his other living at Treeton in the county of York). It was obvious that the two men were very different in their beliefs; Adams standing for everything which Stanley found unpalatable in the Church of England. Again, I'm told from people in the village that there was very little calm but, when it was decided by the diocese to remove Stanley from his post in 1660, there was considerable opposition to the reinstatement of Shoreland Adams and a petition was sent from the village to the patron, Sir George Savile, imploring him to consider reinstating the much-respected Thomas Stanley. I found a copy of the petition which I passed to Edward. The contents of the *'humble petition and certificate'*, signed by no less than sixty-nine freeholders and other villagers of Eyam, stated:

Humbly shewing and declaringe that one Shorland Adams about twenty years since was minister at Eyam aforesaid and that duringe the tyme hee continued as minister there your petitioners well knows and humbly certifie that the said Mr Adams was scandalous in life, negligent and

*idle in preachinge, of a turbulent and Contentious spirit and proud
behaviour, to our great prejudice and discouragement; with all of which
your honourable father was well acquainted and declared himselfe much
displeased with the Carriage and Course of life of the said Mr Adams, for
which Cause and for that the said Mr Adams then held and enjoyed the
parsonage of Treeton in the County of Yorke, the said Mr Adams shortly
afterwards left Eyam, and being then destitute of a minister, through
the mercy of God, and assistance of our friends, we procured one Mr
Thomas Stanley an able, peaceable pyous orthodox Devine to be our
minister, who hath Continued with us ever since and Diligently Carefully
and Constantly hath preached and taught amongst us, by whose pyous
preachinge and painefull instruction wee have received much comfort to
our Soules, and by the good Example of his holy and peaceable life are
much encouraged.*

*Wherefore wee humbly beseech your honour (beinge informed that it
is in your power only) to Continue and settle the said Mr Stanley to be
our minister at Eyam aforesaid and thereby you will bring much glory
to God and Comfort to our Soules, and for which wee shall ever prayse
God and pray for your honour's happiness.*

But their petitioning was not successful and on a designated day, St
Bartholomew's Day in 1662, Stanley (in common with many similarly
minded priests of his persuasion) resigned the living. This was precipitated
by the Act of Uniformity and the introduction of the new Book of
Common Prayer during that year. If Stanley was to stay true to his beliefs
and principles, then it was clearly impossible for him to remain in post.

When talking with Edward, I conceded that, perhaps because of the
great difference in our age, Stanley certainly had a benign and calming
influence on many of the parishioners in this divided congregation, but
I also had to own that our differences in belief and churchmanship have
caused their own continuing conflict. Since being inducted into the parish,
Stanley's unseen influence is still palpable – although I believe that, at base,
he has the same hopes for the well-being of the people within this divided
and much-troubled community. Perhaps the time approaches, or indeed is
imminent, that we should (in light of the absence of others in the parish)
discuss the troubled times which we are now living through, and how best
we can initiate actions that may help to mitigate its further devastating
effects. In order to support this assertion I made reference to the fact that,
as the contagion grows, people are beginning to bury their dead as soon as
is humanly possible. Edward confirmed that from the best evidence he'd
heard, from London's most recent turmoil, this action helps to stop the
infection from leaving the body and entering into the general atmosphere.

Indeed, some Londoners are now burying their dead at depths of up to six feet in the hope that the plague seeds will not rise from the tomb. Here at Eyam, villagers only having small plots of land have sought permission to bury their dead in the croft at the Miners' Arms, whilst others are digging graves in Cucklett Delph and on the grounds behind the church.

I acknowledged the wisdom of Edward's advice, and agreed to his suggestion that I should meet with the Revd Stanley to discuss and agree a joint course of action.

Extract from the Journal of the Revd William Mompesson:
Saturday 22 June 1666

Following the advice from my brother-in-Christ, Edward, I held a second meeting with the Revd Stanley this morning. As with our earlier amicable and constructive meeting, we met in my study; a room well-known to both of us and in which we both feel comfortable and at ease. We honed and finalised the ideas which we'd discussed earlier in the week. We're aiming to present details of our suggestions, which, hopefully, will limit the effects of this terrible pestilence, to a public meeting in the near future, possibly following Divine Worship on Sunday.

In discussing the measures which we needed to take in order to try to ensure the containment of the plague, I'd first suggested to the Revd Stanley that we should immediately cease formal funerals within the village and also curtail burial of the dead in the church grounds. I suggested this for purely practical reasons as it was becoming impossible for the sexton to cope with the influx. The Revd Stanley agreed with this proposal. I added, on a more humane note, I, together with Mrs Mompesson, considered that our time would be better spent, and the people of the village better served, if we comforted the dying and bereaved as well as assisting, where necessary, with the preparation of wills. At this juncture, the Revd Stanley suggested that this was a most important commitment and that he personally wished to be involved, not only in the ministry to the sick and dying, if I could allow this to be, but also in the preparation of wills and wishes. He added that he had some considerable experience of this, and together with his brother, John, who was an attorney over at Chesterfield, he believed that he could be of service in this regard. When considering the actual committal we came to the conclusion that it might be better to suggest that close relatives should be responsible for the burial of their own family members and that burial should be on their own land, preferably within their gardens or orchards. Knowing that, because of the increasing number of deaths, time was becoming a more critical factor, we concluded that our earlier thought of holding the public meeting after tomorrow's service of Divine Worship was indeed the most appropriate time.

Following this initial agreement, I went on to suggest that the next aspect of containment that we should consider was the manner in which the disease was spread. The Revd Stanley commented that we were unsure as to how the disease multiplied, but he did agree to the second measure which was to lock the church until the plague departed the village and that Divine Worship should be held in the open air.

Finally, we broached the most difficult part of our discussions, which was to agree that, in an attempt to control the extent of the pestilence, we needed some form of quarantine; this was considered by both of us to be the only way of containment. The Revd Stanley stated that when similar measures had been taken elsewhere, notably areas in and around London, the enforcement had proved to be less than effective. He did concede, however, that most of the villagers within the parish were in a completely different situation from people in London, in that it would be difficult, if not impossible, for them to relocate to kinsfolk outside of the village. I do believe that a quarantine can be sustained here, due in the main to peoples' stoicism and their faith in the Almighty.

From my time at Scalby, I was aware of the system which they had adopted when a similar pestilence had befallen that place. Money for provisions was left in vinegar-filled holes which had been drilled into stone slabs at the delivery and collection points. A similar system could be adopted here at the Eyam Boundary Stone, where holes could be drilled into the stone and money placed therein. I believe that by using this method, the seeds of the plague would be washed from the coins, thus rendering it safe for others to handle. The system used at Bakewell at Mondaybrook is a little different, in that payment is left in running water, but this, I am told, has the same cleansing effect and the seeds of plague are removed from the coins.

From the Diary of Catherine Mompesson:
Sunday 24 June 1666

After morning worship had concluded, I stayed, with Beth, for the public meeting which was held in order to discuss, together with some other matters, the possibility of a *cordon sanitaire* around the village in order to try to stop or at least curtail the spread of the pestilence to surrounding villages. The meeting was well attended, with many non-worshippers joining the throng after the service had ended. Looking around, I made the comment to Beth that it would be difficult to predict the outcome of the meeting, as there was still some resentment as to William's role within the parish, but considering that the Revd Stanley was now stood at his side, perhaps he would gain the support which would be necessary to carry the day.

During the meeting, which lasted well over an hour, many searching questions were asked, and it was clear that there were many misgivings in the parish as to the wisdom of taking these decisions. However, with many timely interventions from the Revd Stanley, all of the recommendations were agreed to – albeit in some cases with a marked degree of uncertainty and apprehension. With regards to the *cordon sanitaire* there was a certain degree of rancour which, again, the Revd Stanley was able to diffuse by giving a personal assurance that it was his deeply held belief that a *cordon sanitaire* was the most effective method a containing and, hopefully, curtailing the pestilence.

The final decisions reached were as follows; as of now, there would be no funerals within the village, and burials would not take place in the church graveyard, but in land owned by the family of the deceased person; as from Sunday next, the service of Divine Worship would be held away from the church; and finally, and most contentiously, a *cordon sanitaire* would circle the village, and nobody would move outside of this prescribed area. There were many related questions as to who would patrol the perimeter, and where the provisions would be obtained from. William answered all of these questions, and stated that, during the coming week, he would have a further reconnoitre of the perimeter and, before Sunday next, would ensure that everyone in the village knew of the boundaries and also the places where provisions would be left. He also agreed to write to the Earl of Devonshire to seek his assistance and, again, this information would be made available to all.

From the Diary of Catherine Mompesson:
Monday 25 June 1666

It was another bright summer's day yesterday so, after evening prayer, William and I walked over the fields and up along the footpath behind the rectory. It's a walk that we often do and with all of the events which had occurred during the day, especially now that so many people of influence have departed the parish, the burthen of responsibility is lying heavily on William's shoulders. I know William finds that our walks are proving to be a time for him to relax and also afford him some much-needed time for contemplation and reflection. During our walk, which took us up almost as far as Wright's wood, William confided that he had already written to the Earl of Devonshire outlining his plans and proposed course of action. He also revealed that, so as not to 'muddy the waters', he had not made reference in the letter to the role which was being played, and was to be played, by the Revd Stanley. For the same reason, he had not retained a copy of the letter. He was hopeful of a response from the Earl sometime before the end of the week.

Much as William is cognizant of his need of the Revd Stanley, I know that he is also troubled at the duplicity which he is consciously condoning in allowing a Nonconformist minister to perform such an important role within the parish. There is turmoil and anguish in William's heart – knowing, as he does, that without the support and selfless assistance which the Revd Stanley is giving, then much of the work could not be coped with and, perhaps more significantly, the ultimate outcome of yesterday's village meeting might have been very different. William said very little on our walk back to the rectory; I know that he misses the children almost as much as I do.

From the Diary of Catherine Mompesson:
Tuesday 26 June 1666

However much I try to concentrate on each day's tasks, I find that my mind invariably remains fixed on the events of Sunday. I still recall looking around the church during William's sermon. It was clear that there was doubt etched in the minds of many of the congregation as to the import of what he was saying, but the text which he had chosen was more than apt; from John 15:13: 'Greater love hath no man than this, that he lay down his life for his friends'. William gave further emphasis to his text afterwards at the public meeting and then, supported by the Revd Stanley who at this point was standing by his side, we knew that the measures which they were suggesting would be adopted. It is certainly a bizarre work of Fate that throws together the former Nonconformist rector of the parish and William, both of whom are now working for the common good in this turbulent village. The fact that they now face the peoples' problems together has undoubtedly cemented the acceptance of their plan across the entirety of the parish; ranging from those adhering to the now re-established Church of England to the differing, if private, beliefs of the parishioners who formerly followed Puritan and Nonconformist beliefs.

Even though William had suggested that, to minimise the fear of the spread of the contagion, people should now bury their own kinsfolk in their gardens or orchards, some, I believe, had already begun to do so and that was even before Marshall Howe took upon himself the role of self-appointed plague sextant.

William had also suggested that, because it was known that the disease spread when people were in close proximity to one another, it would be better to hold services of Divine Worship in the open air, thus allowing people to stand or pray at some distance from one another. It was held that Divine Worship was still an important aspect of village life and that, having agreed to the church being locked, services should forthwith be held at Cucklett Delph.

There had been one major problem which had caused some concern during the meeting and that was, because of the imposition of the *cordon sanitaire*, there would still be the need to obtain certain provisions from outside of the village. Although many parishioners have small plots of land which are almost sufficient to meet their daily needs, others, principally those employed in the lead-mining industry would find difficulty in sustaining themselves and their families. William and the Revd Stanley resolved this problem by giving a categorical assurance that people would not starve, and William said that he would write to the Earl of Devonshire.

From the Diary of Catherine Mompesson:
Wednesday 27 June 1666

After having breakfast earlier than usual this morning, I sat in the dining room reflecting yet again on the momentous decisions taken last Sunday. Even at this early hour, William is already in deep discussions with the Revd Stanley; I am aware that since those decisions were taken, another three parishioners have died, including Anne Skidmore, who died on Sunday morning some time after the service of Divine Worship; then Jane Townend died on Monday, her mother, widow Anne Townend, having been taken from us just last week; and then, on his return last night, William told me that Emmott Heald had died during the day. I had taken medication to the Healds' home some weeks ago when Emmott's younger sister, Mary, had been taken by the plague, but all to no avail, as she had died eleven days ago.

The impact and ramifications of the decisions are now beginning to sink into peoples' consciousness as, since Sunday, many parishioners have commented on both the practical difficulties, which are arising as a result of those decisions, and also the price which, ultimately, they may have to pay for their courage. It is undoubtedly a very difficult time for everyone, and not least William and the Revd Stanley who, I believe, are suffering from anguish and as a result, both now have some misgivings as to the correctness of the decisions, especially the decision relating to the *cordon sanitaire*. It is a terrible burthen which has now been placed upon them, albeit of their own volition.

The atmosphere in the rectory is becoming oppressive, and I sense that Beth and Edward are also touched by the pervasive air of despondency. It was for this reason that I ventured to suggest to Beth that we should go for a short walk and perhaps look at one of the new boundaries to the village – the southern boundary stone. As Edward was proposing to spend the morning in the parish with William and the Revd Stanley, Beth and I set off alone in the general direction of Stoney Middleton. We walked down the main street from the rectory and made our way to Lydgate. There was an uneasy quiet about the place, so different from when we'd walked down here shortly after Beth and Edward had arrived in our parish. From Lydgate we made our way to the footpath which runs from the village through to Stoney Middleton. We walked through a number of fields and then, after skirting the area around Cliff Stile Mine, we walked across the common land, from where we were rewarded with good views of the village below us. Even now some of the initial effects of the decisions can be seen here, in that some parishioners are fleeing the village but still remaining within the prescribed boundaries of the *cordon sanitaire*, and erecting habitations here.

Since coming to the parish, I have made acquaintance with many people from the village of Stoney Middleton but, until the *cordon sanitaire* is lifted, I will not be able to renew those friendships.

Our footpath then continued directly across more fields, until we reached a number of trees, where we located the large sandstone boulder which had been designated as being the 'boundary stone'. The stone itself already had a number of holes bored into its upper surface. I was aware that money for provisions would be deposited into these vinegar holes, thus purifying it before being removed by the people supplying the provisions. In this way, there would be no fear of the money becoming infected, and thus spreading the contagion. I believe that, in addition to this boundary stone, bread is to be brought over from Wet Withins and also, so I'm told, from Little Common.

We rested for some little while at the boundary stone before returning to the rectory.

Extract from the Journal of the Revd William Mompesson:
Thursday 28 June 1666

Before making my morning visit to the home of Heald family, where Emmott died on Tuesday past, I had much conversation with the Revd Stanley who informed me that earlier this week, also on Tuesday 26 June, Rowland Mower, the cask and barrel maker, had made his last will and Testament. Further, the document was compiled by the Revd Stanley's brother, Joseph Stanley, who is an attorney in Chesterfield. The will bears the mark of Rowland Mower and was witnessed by the Revd Thomas Stanley, Joseph Stanley and William Ainsworth. For completeness, I have appended a transcribed copy of this Last Will and Testament to this journal:

In the Name of God Amen. The sixe & twentieth day of June Ano dnj 1666 I Rowland Mower of Eyam in the county of Derby, Cooper, beinge of good & pfect memory and Vnderstandinge. (blessed be God for it) but consideringe God Almightys heavy visitation vpon this Towne of Eyam, & vpon my owne Family at this psent: Doe make & ordaine this my last will and Testamt in manner & forme following: vizt First and principally I doe bequeath & resigne vp my soule into the hands of Almight God: Hopeing through the merits of Jesus Christ my Saviour & Redeemer to inherit eternal life: And my body to the earth: when it shall please the Lord to call me hence: to be interred according to the discretion of my friends: And as for such Worldly Estate as well Real as Psonall as it hath pleased the Lord to endowe me withall, I doe give, bequeath & dispose thereof as followeth, vizt Impr. I doe give & bequeath vnto John Torre of Eyam aforesayd my brother in Law the sume of tenne shillings of Lawful English money: Item. I doe give & bequeath vnto Robt. Masland my naturall brother tweluepence: Item. I doe give & bequeath vnto Elizabeth the wife of Henry Clarke my naturall Sister the sume of tenne shillings of like lawful English money: Ite. I doe give, bequeath, & leave the sum of fforty shillings of like lawful English money, to be putt forth shortly after my decease, into safe hands for the use & behalfe of the poore of the towne of Eyam: And the yearly Interest and Pfit thereof to be distributed at the Feast of the Nativity of our Lord yearly to the most necessitous poore of Eyam towne according to the discretion of the Minister & Overseer of the poore of Eyam aforesayd for ever. Ite. I doe give a bequeath vnto Thomas Bockinge, Robert Bockinge & Edyth Bockinge the children of Francis Bockinge of Eyam aforesayd each of them ffive shillings. Ite. I doe give & bequeath vnto each of the children of James Mower, Thomas Ragge, & William Abell of Eyam aforesayd twelue pence a piece. Ite. I doe give & bequeath vnto Thomas Stanley of Eyam aforesayd Clerke the sume of fforty shillings of like lawful English money: Ite. My will and minde is & I doe by these pesents devise, order, & appoynt That Jane French my Tenant shall have & enjoy the house wherein she now dwelleth, payinge to my heyrs & Assignes at the Feast of Pentecost the yearly rent of twopence (if it be lawfully demanded) for & during the time of her naturall life. The rest of my worldly goods and chattels whatsoever moueable and vnmoueable, quicke and dead, together with all my houses lands & Real Estate (my debts Legacies & funeral expenses first payed and discharged). I doe give, bequeath, & leave vnto Elizabeth my beloved wife, & Rowland my naturall son, & to the longer liuer of them two: That is to say: If It Please the Lord to take away my sayd son Rowland, & my wife to live: Then my will and minde is that she shall haue & enjoy not only my goods and chattels but alsoe all my houses & lands for and duringe the terme of her naturall Life: And if she be now with childe then I doe leave & appoynt the sayd childe, be it son or daughter, to be my lawfull heyre to all my Real estate: And if she bringe forth a man-childe & both it & my son Rowland doe live: Then I doe leave and appoynt them to be co-heyrs to all my houses & lands And my sayd wife to have the moity or one halfe thereof duringe her life as aforesayd: And my sayd son or sons to enter vpon & have the other moity or halfe thereof, when he or they shall accomplish his or their age or ages of one & twenty years: But if my sayd wife depart this life and leave behind her any Issue by me, vnder the age of one & twenty years: Then I do hereby nominate and appoynt Henry Clarke my brother in Law, & Elizabeth his wife my naturall Sister, Guardians over & for such my Issue to manage my Estate for their Education, till they come to age. But if it shall please the Lord to take away both my sayd son Rowland, & my sayd wife without any of my Issue left behinde her: Then my will & minde is, & I do hereby give, bequeath & dispose of all my wordly Estate both Reall & Psonall (besides the Legacies afore bequeathed) as followeth. That is to say. Impr. I doe give & bequeath the sume of six pounds, over & besides the afore bequeathed sume of fforty shillings (that is to say, eight pounds in the whole) to be putt forth shortly after the longer liver of my sayd wife and son by my heyrs Executes & Assignes to be employed, improved, & distributed to & for the poore of the towne of Eyam, according as is before herein mentioned & expressed for ever. Ite. I do give & bequeath vnto George Cooper my true and lawfull Apprentice the sume of Four pounds beinge the sume which his father Abraham Cooper gave me with him to be returned to him together with his indentures for his best Advantage frome & after the decease of my sayd wife & son. Ite. I doe give & bequeath vnto Hannah Cocker my Niece the Tenant-right of my house with the Apptnces in Froggatt. Ite. I doe give & bequeath vnto John Torre my brother in Law aforesayd all my cowper-wares wood & tools whatsoever: And alsoe all that my Close or peel of land enclosed, comonly called & knowne by the name of Shininge-cliffe in Eyam aforesayd, for & duringe only the terme of the naturall life of him the sayd John Torre: And the rest of all my wordly Estate as well Reall as Psonall together with the Revertion, Inheritance & Remainder of the sayd close called Shining-cliffe I doe give bequeath & leave vnto my naturall Sister Elizabeth Clarke aforenamed, for and during the terme of

her naturall life: And afterwards vnto Jonathan Cocker, George & John
Clarke her three sons equally amongst them, and their heyrs for euer. And
lastly I doe nominate & appoynt Elizabeth my sayd wife & Henry Clarke
my brother in Law, Joyntly & Severally Executes of this my last will &
Testam. to Pforme all things herein mentioned to my intente: And I do
hereby revoke & make void all former wills: And this only to be my last
Will & Testam. In witness I have putt my hand and Seale ye day & year
first above written.

Rowland Mower
his X marke.

Sealed, signed & delivered in the presence of us

Tho: Stanley
Jo: Stanley,
William Ainsworth.

From the Diary of Catherine Mompesson:
Sunday 1 July 1666

Divine Worship was celebrated, for the first time, in Cucklett Delph
this morning. It was certainly very different from our normal service,
but appeared to have been met with general approval from most of the
families present. After the service, William held a short meeting to inform
everyone about the services which he was proposing to hold. There
would be services on Wednesdays and Fridays, in addition to the two
Sunday services. I know that William will be unwavering in preaching
his constant message of life and hope. Before the meeting ended, he also
informed all of those present of the letter which he had received from
the Earl of Devonshire. He was able to report that not only had the
Earl forwarded some plague remedies, which had been used at court,
but he had also magnanimously agreed to supply both food and medical
supplies at his own expense. The agreed collection point would be at the
southernmost boundary of the village but the times for collection and
delivery still needed to be agreed, as the Earl could not run the risk of
the possibility of infection crossing when deliveries were being made. I
suspect that at this point I could hear one or two cynical voices suggesting
that the Earl was supplying the comestibles as a safeguard against his
estates becoming infested, but I chose to ignore these fallacious and
malicious comments.

It was impressed upon the villagers that any further provisions, which they may require, would have to be made known and these items paid for by themselves. Two other collection points were designated, one on the hills above Eyam. Some supplies would be coming from as far away as Fulwood, which is quite near to Sheffield, and these goods were to be left at the point which, overnight almost, has become known colloquially as Mompesson's Well – this area lies by the road to Grindleford and is some way outside of our village. The other, more distant point, is at Wet Withens on Eyam Moor. People from the tiny village of Bubnell, near to Baslow, will be providing bread. I am told that there are also some near neighbours at Stoney Middleton and Foolow who, having relatives at Eyam, will be donating provisions at their own expense.

As I later remarked to Beth, on reflection it seems that 1664, the year when William was inducted into the parish, was truly a significant year. We were blessed with the birth of our daughter, Elizabeth, and then William was given the living when the former rector of the parish, the Revd Shoreland Adams, died on 11 April. Also in that momentous year, the wife of the Revd Stanley, the former Puritan rector, died on 14 June. Grieving over the death of his dear wife and seeking refuge and succour, the Revd Stanley had now returned to the village.

On looking around, my heart was filled with lines from Psalm 121, 'I will lift up mine eyes unto the hills, from whence cometh my help' and that gave me succour to continue with this wretched burthen.

From the Diary of Catherine Mompesson:
Tuesday 3 July 1666

Yesterday, during one of their regular meetings, the Revd Stanley had informed William that Deborah Elliott, who lived with her widowed aunt Jane Naylor, was now gravely ill. I made it my business to visit their home this morning to see if I could be of any assistance. On my way through the village I met Robert Slynn. During our brief conversation I asked as to the well-being of his wife, Elizabeth, and their young daughter, Anne; knowing that the plague had struck not too far from their dwelling. Robert, whose widowed father still lived in the village, said that they were all well, and keeping clear of any unnecessary contact, but he did disclose that his wife's father, George Darby, looked as though he was sickening. Learning that George Darby and his wife, Mary, were not in possession of any medicaments, I said that I would take some over on the morrow.

When I arrived at widow Naylor's home, I found that Deborah Elliott had died earlier this morning, and had already been buried by Marshall Howe.

Returning to the rectory I went straight to William's study – a practice which I would not normally adopt, especially as I could hear that he was in discussion with the Revd Stanley. I told of the death of Deborah Elliott and also of my encounter with Robert Slynn. However, as I'd just seen George Darby's wife leaving the rectory, I knew that William was cognizant of George Darby's illness. William said that Mary Darby had asked for either himself or the Revd Stanley to visit their home, as her husband was now dangerously ill and desirous of making his Last Will and Testament.

Before taking his leave of the rectory, William asked me to visit the home of the Lowe family, as he was of the belief that they had a two-year-old son, Joshua, who was in need of caring.

Extract from the Journal of the Revd William Mompesson:
Tuesday 3 July 1666

I spent a goodly period during the morning with the Revd Stanley, during which time we discussed the reaction of the parishioners to the closing of the church, and the new meeting place for Divine Worship. He told me, by talking to people in the village, that the general consensus was that, although it was not comparable with the church itself, most of the congregation felt far safer in the open air. He went on to say that he had visited the home of the Lowe family earlier this morning where William and Ellenor Lowe had both died yesterday, leaving their three remaining children to look after themselves. I was aware that their eldest daughter, Sarah, had died sometime last month. The Revd Stanley had also been told that two of the other children, Elizabeth and Anne, were also showing some initial symptoms of having contracted the pestilence.

Towards the end of our discussions, Mrs Mary Darby was shewn into the study. She stated that, because her husband, George Darby, had now been smitten by the contagion, he was desirous for either myself or the Revd Stanley, to assist in drafting his Last Will and Testament. I assured her that one of us would call round later in the day.

As she left, Mrs Mompesson came into the study and informed us of the death Deborah Elliott. She also told of George Darby's illness but, having just seen Mrs Darby leaving, realised that we were already aware of this news.

Before departing, for the home of Mr and Mrs Darby, I asked Catherine if she could pay a visit to the home of the Lowe family, where Mr and Mrs Lowe had just died. The Revd Stanley had said that, in addition to their two daughters, he thought that the family also had a two-year old son, Joshua.

I did not tarry over the writing of George Darby's last will and testament, as it was all too obvious that he is not of this world for very much longer. Darby, a relatively wealthy man by Eyam standards, desired that his lead mine should be divided, equally, between his wife, Mary, and his young daughter, also called Mary. He also wished for the turn-trees and other mining tools to be shared equally between them.

Extract from the Journal of the Revd William Mompesson:
Wednesday 4 July 1666

I learnt that George Darby had died in the early hours of this morning; indeed, not too long after I had left him.

From the Diary of Catherine Mompesson:
Wednesday 4 July 1666

After last Sunday's service of Divine Worship, which was the first to be held at Cucklett Delph, Beth and I had agreed to have a further reconnoitre of the place. However, before venturing there again today, I had first to visit the home of the Lowe family where William and Ellenor Lowe had died on Monday. I was aware that their daughters, Elizabeth and Anne, were both suffering from the plague, but I did not know the state of health of the couple's baby son, Joshua. After administering a new plague remedy, we enquired as to the whereabouts of baby Joshua, only to be told that, before the *cordon sanitaire* had been agreed, their parents had had the baby taken over to kinsfolk in the next valley.

We left the house, promising to return with more comestibles before the end of the week. We then made our way through to the Delph. Having more time to gain a better impression of the place, we found that the area has a number of limestone outcrops, and that the Delph itself forms a natural amphitheatre. I believe that the area was known to the church wardens previously, and it was they who suggested the area as being ideal, as it would allow for the congregation of family groupings to be kept at a safe and discrete distance from one another, while maintaining the cohesion so necessary for village worship. We noticed that, in addition to the limestone outcrops, the Delph is crossed by streams, and there are ample verdant slopes upon which the congregation can be seated; there's even a rock which I'm sure William could put to use as a pulpit, and from there lead his people in worship.

I commented to Beth how dramatically things have changed in such a short time. It's unquestionably true that a lot has happened to us over the last few years, and certainly since we left Scalby to come here. Our children are now growing fit and healthy, albeit at some distance, and we have a lot to be thankful for; I suppose our own destiny has been mirrored in events which have occurred since the restoration of the monarchy, which now seems a lifetime ago in 1660. Much is due to the number of acts of parliament which have been passed since that time, many relating to the established church and dissenting clergy. I know full well that the Revd Thomas Stanley is now officially banned from holding public office and that any meetings for worship which he does attend outside of the order of the Church of England are actually illegal. William also tells me that he is forbidden to preach within a five-mile radius of this parish but I don't know whether that ruling is being strictly adhered to, as the Earl of Devonshire could have enforced the terms of this parliamentary act but he appears to be sanguine and accepting of the fact that the Revd Stanley is residing in our parish; and, following the introduction of the 1662 Book of Common Prayer, shortly before we arrived here, I also know full well that the Revd Stanley has not taken the oath to obey its teachings. Like many others, he resigned his living on St Bartholomew's Day in 1662.

From the Diary of Catherine Mompesson:
Thursday 5 July 1666

I first encountered John Carter on the morning following his summoning of Marshall Howe to give his ministrations to his near neighbour, Edward Unwin. Although Carter never made reference to his neighbour's Christian name, and for all I know he may not even have been aware of it, but, because of his attendance at Sunday worship, I knew that he was called Edward. Carter himself was unkempt and feral in appearance, his sharp features being accentuated by a shock of soot black hair. Unlike Howe, Carter was short in stature but he too was sturdily built. He was reputed to be thirty-four years of age, but, no doubt due to his activities at the mine, looked some ten years older. Like many of the other lead-miners, he was direct and honest in his conversation but there was a certain jocose air about him as he related the story of the previous day.

   Knowing that Unwin was either dead or on the verge of death, Carter summoned his fellow-miner Marshall Howe, the self-appointed sexton of the plague, to Unwin's dwelling on the western side of the village, the so-called Town Head. After taking a cursory glance at the possessions which Howe would be able to claim as a result of his ministrations to the dead widower, he checked the location of the body before immediately starting to dig a shallow grave in Unwin's orchard which was directly behind the dwelling. The air was cleaner in the orchard, with a gentle aroma of ripening apples; very different from the putrid smell of death and disease lifting from the earthen floors in the cottage. Having completed his unsavoury task, Howe wasted no time in returning to the room where the body lay so as to draw this day's work to a close and return to his home with the spoils of his endeavours, before darkness fell once again over the village. Now quite accustomed and, apparently, immune to the pestilence, Howe mounted the stairs and lifted the body over his back without any undue ceremony; he'd conducted similar duties on numerous occasions by now and viewed every burial as a mere task to be completed as quickly as humanly possible. Halfway down the stone steps, a groan emanated from the still warm body. Howe thought nothing of it, attributing it to the movement of air within the spent trunk. But then, before reaching the bottom of the stairs, there was a distinct cry from the 'corpse', declaring 'I want a posset!' Without taking further thought, Howe unburthened himself of his charge and vacated the premises with unseemly haste! John Carter, still chuckling to himself, went on to tell me that Edward Unwin received his posset, a mixture of boiled milk, ale, bread and other ingredients, from a neighbour, and is showing every sign of recovery.

Further, and according to local gossip I've heard around the village, it is reputed that in his zeal to complete his self-appointed task, Marshall Howe might have committed other people to an early grave, without there being a need to do so! I haven't mentioned this rumour to William, as he might become perplexed and that certainly wouldn't ease his already arduous burthen.

Extract from the Journal of the Revd William Mompesson:
Saturday 7 July 1666

One of the neighbours of widow Elizabeth Swann came to the rectory this morning, and informed me that she had died and been buried by Marshall Howe yesterday; and this is just one week since her son, John, was taken by the plague.

From the hand of Beth Hounsfeild:
Sunday 8 July 1666

As we were sat at the breakfast table this morning, the maid came in and said that the Revd Stanley was waiting in the study and needed to see William on urgent parochial business; this was very much out of the ordinary as normally on a Sunday William would not meet up with the Revd Stanley until after the service of Divine Worship.

On William's return, he informed us that John Townend, Jane's younger brother, had died yesterday, as had Anne Talbot, one of the daughters of Richard Talbot of Riley; this follows the death of her sisters Bridget and Mary who both died on Thursday. Catherine suggested that, when time permitted, we should visit the Talbots and also, possibly, the Hancocks who live adjacent; and to think, it was only just over a week ago when we walked as far as the boundary stone. In the short time that has elapsed, there have been fourteen more deaths.

This afternoon William told us that, during the day, another child of the parish had died, widow Ragge's nine-year-old daughter, Francis Ragge. He also said that he'd visited the Thorpe household where Elizabeth was gravely ill and not expected to survive the night.

CHAPTER FIVE
TRAGEDY AT RILEY

Extract from the Journal of the Revd William Mompesson:
Tuesday 10 July 1666

During the past few days we've had many more deaths in the parish. Since the start of the month there have been seventeen souls lost to the plague. First, there was Elizabeth Heald on 1 July and then William and Ellenor Lowe the following day. In truth, there hasn't been a day in the week past when one or more of our steadily dwindling flock hasn't fallen victim. I've endeavoured, as far as is humanly possible, to visit the dying and bereaved, more often than not being accompanied by my brother-in-Christ, the Revd Thomas Stanley.

Two of the Talbot sisters died on Thursday, as did Anne Coyle and John Daniel, and then on Saturday Anne Talbot, Richard's five-year-old daughter, also died. Sometime afterwards I visited the stricken household where, before leaving, Richard dictated his last will and testament. I've omitted to record the date of this particular visit, and therefore the exact date of the making of the will, but it has been within the last two or three days. Parochial duties are such that the hours and even the days are now beginning to merge into one continuous round of visitations. My dear wife and helpmate is proving to be a tireless companion without whom I would find it virtually impossible to sustain the fortitude to continue my God-given task. In addition to her household duties in the rectory, Catherine often accompanies me on visits when the Revd Stanley is occupied on other work in the parish. In parenthesis, I would also add that Catherine's cousin, Beth, and her husband, Edward, have been a great comfort, opting to continue to reside here in these troubled and turbulent times.

As is becoming my accustomed practice, I am appending to this journal a copy of Richard Talbot's last will and testament.

In ye name of God Amen, I Richard Talbot of Ryley in ye County of Derby Yeoman, being sick and weak but in good memory, do make this my last will and testament in manner and forme following. First I bequeath my soul into ye hands of God who made me, depending my salvation upon the account of Jesus Christ my Redeemer, my body to be buried at the discretion of my Executor. My estate I dispose as followeth.

First I give all my estate to my loving wife Catherine Talbot (if she marry not again) but if she should marry again a third part of my estate only, out of which fair estate she is to give my eldest son Robert Talbott a heifer called Buxton heifer: and the smithy shop to George Talbott my son paying upon the day of his marriage five pounds to the said Robert Talbott. If the said George dye then the smithy shop to go to Jonathan my third son, if all my children dye then I give my whole estate to be divided equally between Jonathan Hunstone of Ashton under Lyne in ye County of Lancashire and Joseph Bramhall of Ryley aforesaid to be equally divided between them and if the said Joseph dye then his moyety to be distributed among the poor of Eyam parish according to the discretion of my executor and lastly I make William Mompesson Rector of Eyam Executor of this my last will and Testament witness my hand and this of July 1666.

Rich: T. Talbott
his marke

Sealed & signed
in ye presence of

Rob: R. Fydler
his marke

Fran: F. Blackwell
his marke

From the hand of Beth Hounsfeild:
Wednesday 11 July 1666

I met the Revd Stanley as he was just leaving the rectory early this afternoon. Since Divine Worship was moved from the church, I haven't had an opportunity to talk with him about the new meeting place, and I know that Catherine is still harbouring some misgivings. The Revd Stanley set my mind at rest and reassured me that most of the parishioners, with whom he had had contact since that time, were, in general, in favour of the move. As he was about to take his leave, he related an incident which had occurred sometime last week. Apparently, a woman – whose name he hadn't been given, but who lived at the Town Head, in one of the houses that stand away from the road, near to the raised footpath – had witnessed other families leaving the village. She too was desirous of leaving the parish, having seen so many in recent weeks either having fled the village or died within its bounds. She had walked the five miles over to Tideswell to make her entrance into the town unnoticed and was then intent on spending her days in safety living there. She knew that on market day the population of the small town would be swollen by an influx of visitors; pedlars, market traders, dairy maids selling poultry, eggs, butter and cheese, and farmers from outlying villages trading livestock. But first, in order to enter the town, she had to negotiate her way past the parish constable.

The town authorities, being fully aware of the contagion at Eyam, had instituted rigorous procedures to prevent the plague entering their town. A constable had been posted at the eastern entrance to keep watch and ward; his purpose here being to interrogate any visitors who looked to be arriving from the general direction of Eyam. Upon approaching the check point, the woman was duly stopped and the guard asked, 'Woman, whence comest thou?' to which she gave the honest answer that she came from Orchard Bank, for that was the locality in Eyam from whence she came. But the guard, being unaware of specific areas in the village, questioned her further, asking, 'And where is that?', whereupon she replied in biblical terms, stating, 'Why, verily, 'tis in the land of the living!' Her disarming answer was enough to convince him that she posed no problem, and allowed her to enter the town. But, barely had she reached the market when she was recognised by another woman who, startled, uttered the cry 'the plague! the plague! – a woman from Eyam!' In a state of shock at having been identified, she was soon surrounded by a baying crowd and pelted with anything that readily came to hand; sods of turf, stones, sticks, mud and other, unmentionable, missiles, before being pursued for upwards of a mile out of the market place by the incensed townsfolk. The Revd Stanley said that when she eventually did arrive back at the village, she was much chastened and a 'sadder but wiser woman'.

It would clearly be a difficult task to ensure that the *cordon sanitaire* was maintained and thus served its purpose. I have to own that I am not convinced that it was the right decision, but only time will tell. I have not voiced these opinions to either Edward or Catherine, and certainly not to William.

From the hand of Beth Hounsfeild:
Wednesday 18 July 1666

William was in a jocular mood when he related news which had been received in the village this morning. Seemingly, a carter from Bubnell, a village a mile or two from here and adjacent to Baslow, was plying his normal trade. Because there was a shortage of wood in the area, he'd been asked to deliver a load of wood from the Earl of Devonshire's estate at Chatsworth, to some of the nearby villages. But, as his route passed through Eyam, nobody from the village would accompany him on his foolhardy mission. Indeed, his family and neighbours, aware of the potentially hazardous journey he was contemplating, remonstrated with him and implored him not to venture anywhere near to Eyam. But the carter, being a physically strong man, chose to ignore their arguments and exhortations and set off towards Chatsworth. Being alone, it took some time to load the cart, and, when he eventually did reach his final destination, the unloading took even longer since none could be coaxed or cajoled into assisting him, in part because of the route he'd taken back from Chatsworth but also because of the torrential rain which was now falling.

Once his arduous day's work had been completed, the weary carter returned home in his wet clothes. Shortly afterwards he showed symptoms of a chill and developed a slight fever. He took to his bed. When news of the illness spread throughout the village, it was immediately construed as evidence that the carter had taken infection from the plague thus spreading fear and alarm. His neighbours took decisive action, posting a vigilante guard outside of his cottage with strict instructions to raise the alarm should the carter attempt to cross the threshold. It was even rumoured that, in this unlikely event occurring, the guard had permission to shoot him!

News of the carter's condition was also conveyed to the Earl. When he was acquainted with details of the case, and wishing to allay fears, he instructed the messengers to return to their village, stating that his personal physician would visit the village on the morrow, so that a thorough examination of the woebegone individual could take place. No doubt there was a secondary motive, in that the Earl needed to reassure himself of his own continuing security. After all, Bubnell was only two miles from Chatsworth, and, if there was any prospect of the plague spreading any nearer, then clearly it would be time for him and his family to depart and move out of harm's way.

Having been given explicit instructions by the Earl, the doctor was hardly in any position to refuse, although he did exhibit a marked and understandable reluctance to visit any village in the near vicinity of Eyam. The following day he duly arrived in the village but, being fearful of his own mortality, he sent instructions to the carter to leave his house and walk through the village until reaching the bridge which crossed the Derwent. He was then to cross the bridge and continue walking along the river bank. But, rather than follow the hapless carter across, the doctor stationed himself on the eastern bank! Then, by shouting a series of questions across the fast-flowing river, he was able to ascertain that the now suitably chastened and cowed carter was suffering from nothing more than a very heavy cold. He was given a prescription and, following a complete recovery, was duly, but reluctantly, released from the village-imposed quarantine.

It was obvious from the wry smile on William's countenance that the whole episode had occasioned some much-needed light relief. It has been many days since I've seen any humour written on his gaunt face.

From the Diary of Catherine Mompesson:
Thursday 19 July 1666

Today, Beth and I decided to walk over to the home of Robert Heald and his son Thomas. William had told me that Thomas was now suffering from the distemper, and I was aware that his mother, Elizabeth, had died from the plague on the very first day of this month. William and the Revd Stanley had visited the home during June, when both of Thomas's sisters, Mary and Emmott, had died.

I took with me some medicaments to administer and, before leaving the rectory, I made a copy of the new plague remedy which William's fellow clergyman over at Hathersage, the Revd John Walker, had recommended. Knowing that many of the parishioners were obtaining remedies from Humphrey Merrill, I determined to leave a copy for him on my return from the Heald home.

Much to our dismay, when we arrived at the Healds', we were met by Robert Heald who told us that Thomas had died and had been buried last night.

From the hand of Beth Hounsfeild:
Friday 20 July 1666

Considering that we didn't leave the rectory until long after breaking our fast, the sun still hadn't greeted the day as we set off for the Talbot dwelling on the eastern side of the village. The morning sky was dark and foreboding, with ominous and heavily laden clouds. Small droplets of light rain began to fall, brushing a fine mist-like spray against our faces which were also being gently buffeted by the breeze which now prevailed. The dwelling was some distance away and as we walked up the rise out of the village, the sky lightened to reveal a profusion of cranesbill, celandine and daisies on the limestone outcrop. Then, as the path levelled out, we could just see two dwellings in close proximity to one another, one belonging to the Talbot family and the other to the Hancocks. The lane then took us to the edge of the Manchester to Sheffield road, where I couldn't fail to observe how very different the landscape here is from the more familiar sights along the distant banks of the Mersey; but that seems very far away now. I often wonder as to when Edward and I will be able to return to our native Lancashire but for as long as William and Catherine are in need of us, then we will stay; it's God's purpose.

Ever since the outbreak of the pestilence, with the death toll daily rising, Catherine had been engaged with William in tending to the sick and dying. This morning she had asked me accompany her to the home of the Talbots; theirs was a truly tragic and heart-rending story. Earlier in the year Richard's eldest son, John, had died, but not, I'm told, of the plague. But then, at the beginning of the month Richard's daughter Mary died and on the very same day, his daughter from his first marriage, Bridget, died. And then just two days later his five-year-old daughter, Anne, died. On Tuesday of this week, young Jane was taken by the pestilence. And then, on the following day, Richard's second wife, Catherine, died from the plague. Catherine told me that Joan Talbot, Richard's first wife, died in 1639 and that he had remarried in 1643, some twenty-three years ago.

As we came nearer to the dwelling, I noticed that there was a smithy, now-defunct, close to the property. Catherine said that Richard Talbot was a farmer, but that an adjoining plot of land had been purchased by one of his relatives in 1662, upon which he had recently built a smithy; an ideal position, since it was very near to the track leading to Grindleford.

Following his recent visit to the house, William had told us that he was anxious about Richard's well-being, as he was, understandably, showing signs of distress and fatigue. I also gained the impression that the family of Richard's married son was giving some cause for concern. Robert Talbot, a son from Richard's first marriage, Ruth, his wife, and their baby daughter had now moved from the family home, but still lived nearby. We took prescriptions against the plague to both of the Talbot homes. Catherine had boundless supplies, having been given the recipe from a local family who affirmed that it came from the royal household. I made a note of the recipe, which I'll add to my collection when I return home.

Take Redd Sage, herbe of Grasse, Elder leaves and bramble leaves of
either (each) one handfull. Strayne them with a quarte of whyte wyne,
drynke hereof a spoonfull everye morninge for nyne days togeather and

the firste spoonfuls will preserve you for twenty-four dayes, and see the nynth spoonfuls will suffice for the whole year. If the ptie be infected then take with the thing aforesaid Scabious water and Betany water and a little of the best Treakell and it shall, by the grace of God, dryve oute all the venome from the hurte but yf the Botche appeare then take a handfull of Red sagge, Elder leaves, bramble leaves, mustery seed and beate them all together and make thereof a plaster.

I ventured to suggest to Catherine that 'plague water' was another remedy that I'd been told was efficacious as a precaution against infection. This consisted of a compound of a pound each of twenty roots, sixteen flowers, and nineteen seeds, together with an ounce each of nutmeg, cloves and mace. The method was to shred the flowers, bruise the berries and pound the roots and spices. A peck of green walnuts was then added and, after all the ingredients had been mixed together, the concoction was steeped in wine lees and had to be distilled a week later. Catherine said that we could prepare some, if we collected the ingredients later in the day.

Having administered the prescriptions we returned to the rectory, but promised to visit again in the coming week.

Extract from the Journal of the Revd William Mompesson:
Friday 27 July 1666

Earlier in the day, I heard of the recent death of Richard Talbot and, being the sole executor of his last will and testament, I once again ventured to his desolate dwelling at Riley, where I found the following,

A Just and True inventory of all the Goods and Chattles Moveable and immoveable Quick and dead of Richard Talbott of Ryley in the parish of Eyam in the County of Darby Husbandman Deceased

	£	s	d
His purse and Apparell	5	0	0
Fourscore & seaventeene sheepe	23	0	0
five cowes 2 bullocks, 2 oxen & two heifors	23	0	0
three horses	10	0	0
his Corne and hay	26	0	0
A Swine	1	2	0
his pewter and Brafs	4	10	0
a waine carts plowes harowes yoaks teams horse geares and husbandry ware	4	0	0

Seaven stone of wool	3	0	0
A Garner & three Chests	1	13	6
foure paire of Bed stocks	2	10	0
one Ark & a Cubbord	1	10	0
Two tables A hingboard & a forme	0	10	0
three chaires & stooles	0	6	0
tubs, Loomes & Kitts	1	0	0
three spinninge wheeles	0	4	0
Boards & pieces of timber	1	0	0
Iron tooles of severall sorts	1	0	0
A salting kimnell & A ffatt	0	10	0
A paire of Cart legs a hackney sadle 3 shovels	0	10	0
A silver spoone	0	5	0
Linen yarne	1	10	0
his Maynor	1	10	0
Corne sacks & oat bags	0	10	0
A hive of Bees & two quarts of hony	0	15	0
Ffoure strike & a halfe of meale	0	15	0
A Bed Coveringe a Coverlitt a paire of blankits & A Chafs bed	5	0	0
A paire of sheets pillow beers table napkins with other linnens	4	0	0
A bible & a fafsgard	0	10	0
A Muskett a fword a Iron Candlestick	0	11	6
A Landiron Rackets tongs pot hooks with other necessary things	0	10	0
For any thing thats forgotten	0	5	0
	126	7	0

Godfrey Torre
his marke
Robert Slinne
his marke
Robert Heild

I found a second document with the will; it confirmed that land had been bought in 1662 from George Wragg, a local lead-miner, by one of Richard Talbot's relatives. I surmised that it was upon this land that Richard Talbot had recently erected his smithy. I have appended an abridged extract as follows:

This Indenture made Sep. 24 in the 14 Carolus II (1662) between George Ragge of Eyam, myner, of the one part, and Thomas Talbott of Ryeley in

the parish of Eyam of the other part, WITNESSETH, that for the sum
of twenty five shillings ... George Ragge hath sold to the said Thomas
Talbott, his heirs and assigns for ever ... all that Gardensteed lying at the
east end of the dwelling house of the said George Ragge, and now in the
tenure and occupation of the said Thomas Talbott (whereupon he hath
built a smithy) ...

George Ragge
his mark

Sealed and delivered in the presence of

Thomas Bray
David Cowlishaw
and John Chapman
his mark.

From the Diary of Catherine Mompesson:
Tuesday 31 July 1666

Further tragedy has now befallen the, seemingly, God-forsaken Talbot
family. Robert, Richard Talbot's eldest son, was buried on Tuesday of last
week and his young wife, Ruth, just two days later. Richard himself was
buried on Wednesday, the day after his son. This means that, following
the death of Jonathan, Richard's sixteen-year-old son yesterday, the whole
family, save for Robert and Ruth's baby daughter, Catherine, born in April,
have now been consumed by this insatiable pestilence. In the absence of
Marshall Howe's ghoulish ministrations, we can only speculate that it
was John Hancock's wife, Elizabeth, who took charge of the committal,
as it's doubtful if old Mrs Bridget Talbot, being of a great age, could have
coped.

Indeed, William thinks that the Hancocks are taking care of the baby,
since her only remaining relative, her father's brother, George, is, we
believe, working away at the moment.

From the Diary of Catherine Mompesson:
Friday 3 August 1666

Shafts of sunlight beaming through the dining room windows served to
remind me that this is still God's creation, even though there seem to be more

deaths every single day. Even since Sunday last, there have been another twenty-seven deaths; this must surely be the worst week on record. To say that we're living through tumultuous times is a gross understatement.

As the pestilence has now been raging for some considerable time and having exhausted my own limited supply of remedies, I decided to venture towards Town Head and the dwelling of Humphrey and Anne Merrill at Hollins House. I knew that Humphrey, being a herbalist and apothecary, would still have medicaments available for me. As we were talking, young Alice Hancock was shown in; she had been sent by her mother Elizabeth for more plague cures, as her father John was now showing signs of having succumbed to the pestilence – his children, Elizabeth and John, both having died during the early hours of this morning. Humphrey Merrill measured out a quantity of ointment; a concoction of mixed herbs and spices bound together with human body waste. This was not a remedy that I was aware of but Humphrey assured me that it had been efficacious in the past. I returned to the Hancocks' with Alice, where I encountered a scene of utter desolation and grief. Alice's father, John Hancock, was undoubtedly now suffering from the plague, but so too were her elder brother, William, and baby Oner. I administered the ointment to all three, and promised to return on the morrow.

I told William and the Revd Stanley of the Hancocks' plight.

From the Diary of Catherine Mompesson:
Saturday 4 August 1666

Since my diary entry of Tuesday last yet more tragedy has come upon us, as Alexander Hatfield was buried yesterday. It was towards the end of last year that his stepsons, Jonathan and three-year-old Edward, died of the plague; and before that, his journeyman, George Viccars, who was the plague's first victim. Alexander Hatfield had been married for little more than a year; his wife, Mary, who's just thirty-one years of age, has now been widowed twice in her young life; it seems so cruel.

William told me that the Hancocks at Riley have now been afflicted; the pestilence has leeched from the Talbots to their adjoining neighbours, the Hancocks. Elizabeth Hancock buried two of her children yesterday, Elizabeth aged seventeen, and young John, who was just five years old. We had hoped and prayed that, being so far from the village, both families would not be visited by the pestilence but its dolorous tentacles have spread and reached them. Across the dell, in the neighbouring village of Stoney Middleton, people continued to make their daily journeys to the boundary stone to leave supplies of food, but stood, transfixed, and watched aghast as Elizabeth performed her miserable and wretched task, dragging both of the children and burying them in the orchard next to their home. When time allows I will endeavour to visit, taking a new prescription which William has recommended. Since my prescriptions against the pestilence are proving to be quite ineffective, he has informed me of a remedy which has been widely used, apparently to good effect, in the parish of East Retford. In order to ward off the plague, the parishioners had followed their rector's recipe which, when I had mixed the ingredients, I added to my list of cures:

> *In ye time of a plague let the person either infected or fearfull of ye infection, take a pennyworth of Dragon water, a pennyworth of oyle Olive, Mithrodite 1d. and treacle 1d., then take an unyon and fill it full of pepper, w'n you have fcraped it, then roaft it and after that put in to ye liquor and ftrain and drink it in ye morning, and if you take ye same at night lay foap and bay fait to your feet, and fweat upon it and with God's blesfing you fhall recover.*

Edward had also told me of a remedy which had been approved by the College of Physicians. I added this to my list but did not use it for the time being, in the hope that the East Retford cure would prove efficacious.

> *Take a greate onion, hollow it, put in a fig one cut small and a dram of Venice treacle; put it close stopt in wet paper, and roast it in the embers; apply it hot into the tumour, lay three or four, one after another; let one lie three hours.*

From the Diary of Catherine Mompesson:
Tuesday 7 August 1666

As the weather had recanted during the last week, Beth and I decided to walk out as far as Foolow today. It's a long time since we've trodden this path – in fact, I think that it's almost a year since we've walked this way. The mountain pansies were long since past their best, but there was still an abundance of spring sandwort, or leadwort as it's known over here. Beth was unfamiliar with the flower, as the mineral composition of the land around her part of Lancashire is lacking in lead traces, which the sandwort thrives on. About a mile or so out of the village we came to Shepherd's Flatt and knowing that Robert Kempe, widow Kempe's youngest child, had died at the end of last month, I suggested that we called there. When we came along here last September, I recall that we met with Luke and Joan Morten.

Upon arrival, widow Kempe's greeting was affable enough but she nonetheless barred our entry declaring that Elizabeth and Thomas, both in their twenties, were showing the early signs of having caught the plague. Having no remedy readily available, I said that I would return with some on Thursday. Before leaving, I asked as to the well-being of their neighbour, Margaret Morten, who is heavily pregnant with her third child. Widow Kempe said that, as far as she was aware, everything was as it should be and that the baby was due sometime during the next few weeks.

When we arrived back at the rectory, we found William deep in conversation with the Revd Stanley. He had visited the home of the Hancock family, only to find that John Hancock, William, his son, and Oner had all died during the day. William said that he would pay a visit to the widow as soon as his other parish duties allowed.

From the Diary of Catherine Mompesson:
Thursday 9 August 1666

I returned to Shepherd's Flatt, as promised, and entered the room which was unbearably warm. When administering the medicaments to Elizabeth and Thomas, I encountered the tell-tale putrid odour which is the constant companion of the plague. As the buboes have now appeared, widow Kempe knows that the prognosis is not good. She is also fearful for twelve-year-old, Michael, who is also showing the early signs of having succumbed to the distemper.

I walked back to the village with a heavy heart; there seems to be no end to the devastation, desolation and utter destruction which this visitation is wreaking on the parish. So far this month there have been a further twenty-five souls lost to the pestilence.

William paid another visit to the home of the Hancocks today. He went to offer consolation to Elizabeth Hancock, following the recent deaths in her family. Upon arrival, he was told that fourteen-year-old Alice had been buried earlier in the day and also, if these tragedies weren't sufficient, Anne was now in the final throes of the distemper.

Extract from the Journal of the Revd William Mompesson:
Friday 10 August 1666

Today I made a note of the 'memorandum' of Bridget Talbot. She was, I believe, the mother of Mr Richard Talbot of Riley Farm, and relict of the Revd Robert Talbot, Rector of Eyam from 1617 until his death and burial, which was recorded on 20 August 1630. The informal will bequeaths all of her estate to her grandson, George Talbott, the only remaining family member. She did, however, bequeath a Bible to my son, George Mompesson. Her memorandum as recorded is as follows:

> *Memorandum yt Briget Talbott of Eyam in ye County of Darby: Did give*
> *& bequeath all her estate to George Talbott of Eyam aforesaid excepting*
> *a Bible to George Mompefson son to Wm. Mompefson of Eyam Church;*
> *in ye hearing of*

> *Mary M. Darby.*

Later in the day, the Revd Stanley called and deposited a copy of the inventory relating to Rowland Mower's Goods and Chattles which he had just received. I have appended a copy of this inventory below:

> *A full and true Inventery of all the Goods & Chattles Moveable &*
> *Unmoveable, Quick & Dead of Rowland Mower of Eyam in the County*
> *of Derby, Cooper, Deceased on 29 day of July, 1666.*

	£	s	d
His purse and Apparell	5	0	0
Two Horses	2	10	0
Two Cows & heyfer	5	0	0
Five Sheep	1	0	0
Cooper Wood made & unmade	22	8	6
Corne & hay	3	0	0
Cart & Husbandry Ware	0	10	0
Pewter & Brass	2	0	0
Table, Cubbard & 2 Buffet forms	2	0	0
Coffers & Chesses	1	0	0
3 pair Bed Socks	0	13	4
Bed, Clothes & linen	3	0	0
A salting Cinnell with looms tubs & Rits	0	13	4
Chairs, Stooles & Cusheons	0	12	0
Dish bord a Dish Cradle & Dishes	0	5	0
Hand Iron, toasting do., pair of Rackets & tongs	0	5	4
For anything forgotten	0	2	6
	50	0	0

Praysers Names
    Godfrey Torr
    Nicholas Daniel
    James Mower

From the Diary of Catherine Mompesson:
Thursday 16 August 1666

Once again this morning, I found myself walking the now well-worn path up towards Riley. My heart was heavy, as the pestilence has now plumbed new depths. I was aware that, having taken young Elizabeth and John on 3 August, the children's sister Oner, just three years old, had breathed her last during the night of the sixth. Minutes later their father, John Hancock, had also succumbed. Even before dawn had woken the village, William, sixteen, joined his father and sister. When morning did break, Elizabeth once again had to perform the soul-destroying office of sexton, digging the three graves and dragging, with the aid of a towel tied around their feet, each of her loved ones and interring them in their final resting place.

Then, days later, the villagers of Stoney Middleton helplessly witnessed the final interments, that of her last two children, Alice on 9 August and Anne on the following day. So, in just over a week, Elizabeth Hancock has buried her husband and her six children who still lived at Riley. She is now alone at the farm with, I believe, the young baby of Robert and Ruth Talbot.

From Riley I turned and made my way to Shepherd's Flatt, as I'd promised to see how things were with widow Kempe. I found that Michael, her one remaining child, had been buried yesterday. However, Lydia Kempe had more disquieting news to convey; Matthew Morten, her near neighbour, knowing that his wife's time was near, had ventured into the village to seek help during his wife's time of labour but, without exception, the womenfolk of the parish had refused his pleas, knowing that there was plague at Shepherd's Flatt. With his two other children having fallen victims to the pestilence, Matthew was fearful, not only for his wife's imminent period of labour, but also for her general well-being, knowing that the plague was abroad in the home. I could do naught, save to offer medicaments to counter the plague and assistance during the childbirth.

Upon his return to the rectory, I informed William that Anne Wilson, wife of Francis Wilson of West End Cottage, had died yesterday. He, in turn, said that old Bridget Talbot, the wife of the former rector, had also died yesterday. She bequeathed a Bible to our son, George.

CHAPTER SIX
THE DEATH OF CATHERINE MOMPESSON

From the Diary of Catherine Mompesson:
Wednesday 22 August 1666

I awoke early today to another beautiful summer's morning. The dappled sunlight was already streaming through the window, casting shadows in the still darkened chamber. Looking out, there was a mist lying in the fields, like soft white layers of muslin sheeting, partially masking the gentle cerise at the base of the sky, where the blurred sun looked like a flame of wild rose blossom. Outside, there is tranquillity in the countryside yet not in the village, where the pestilence is still raging.

As summer has progressed, the carnage has continued with unremitting vigour and victims are legion. In July, which in itself was the worst month for mortalities to date, fifty-seven dear souls of this village were taken; but the ravages of August are proving to be even more devastating. I think back to the joyous time we celebrated at this Wakestide last year, but this year the contrast couldn't have been more marked. No relatives and friends visited the village and, rather than the festive bells ringing, all that can be heard is the mournful death toll. The festive Sunday came and passed, but no festival was observed. As the month rolls on, the plague claimed its sixty-fourth and sixty-fifth victims yesterday, when Francis Fryth and one-year-old Ruth Morten both died. Ruth's father, Francis Morten, was formerly of Hope parish. He married Anne Blackwell and they lived at Bretton, just outside of the village, together with Anne's unmarried sister, Sarah. Anne died on 31 July, to be followed by her sister on 13 August, and then, just yesterday, his young daughter was snatched from him. William had visited the family sometime after Sarah's death and I had taken plague remedies to the family when baby Ruth developed plague symptoms. I never cease to wonder at the fortitude of the villagers, most of whom have lost one or more members of their family and some of our parish families have been completely annihilated.

But William is ever mindful of the pastoral and medicinal needs of his flock, as indeed is his close colleague, the Revd Thomas Stanley, who from the very beginning of the visitation of this black pestilence has been a constant support to both William and the parishioners, in their work of visiting and comforting the sick and dying. And, because nearly every family has exhausted their medicinal remedies against the plague, William and the Revd Stanley have been dispensing prescriptions to those in need. Over the last few months I, together with my cousin Beth, have made copious amounts of liquor as remedies to ward off the plague, using a goodly number of different recipes.

With the constant pressures placed upon William because of the turbulence which for so long now has engulfed our village, it is becoming increasingly difficult for him to gain any respite from his manifold responsibilities and duties – each task he embraces with unflinching vigour and fortitude. In addition to dispensing medicines he has, more latterly, become increasingly involved, for obvious reasons, in the writing of wills. In this duty he is given abundant support from both the Revd Stanley and his brother, Joseph, who is a practicing attorney over in Chesterfield.

Whenever opportunity arises, especially since our dear children have departed the village, I often try to persuade William to take an evening stroll though the lanes and fields beyond the rectory. We find that we talk of the children as we walk along. Today, although there was still a goodly part of the daylight remaining, there was a light chill now creeping in the air and already the summer sun was beginning to surrender as dusk tinged the edges of the sky and greying clouds rolled in from the direction of the hills above the village. But, after a careworn day, the air was good; I commented to William 'Oh, Mompesson, the air! How sweet it smells!' But, for reasons best known to himself, William's response was very strange indeed. Instead of sharing my delight in the joy of enjoying a summer's evening away from the day to day cares of the parish, he looked at me quite askance and suggested that we head back to the rectory, even though we'd perhaps only been walking for some twenty or twenty-five minutes.

From the hand of Beth Hounsfeild:
Thursday 23 August 1666

When returning from their evening walk on last night, a little earlier than usual, William had a troubled expression on his countenance and cast a searching sideways look at me as he passed through, as I thought, on his way to the study. Catherine followed and walked in without exchanging any greeting which, in itself, was alien to her gentle nature and totally out of character. Some forty minutes elapsed before William rejoined us in the drawing room. He disclosed that Catherine had retired to her bed chamber suggesting that she was weary after working tirelessly in the parish without having any respite, save for her attendance at Divine Worship, twice on Sundays, and her devotions during the week at Cucklett Delph. In the brief conversation that followed, he also confirmed our surmise that Catherine was grieving for the presence of her children, George and Elizabeth, having now being separated from them for upwards of two months. It was a burthen that was becoming increasingly difficult for her to bear. William then retired to his study; a place of solitude, contemplation and consideration.

This morning, William revealed that Catherine had a slight fever and would be remaining in her chamber until it had subsided. During that day he never left the rectory and hardly ventured from her side, only leaving her to secure additional supplies of cordials and plague remedies. However, on one such occasion he did confide in me and disclosed that he had been deeply troubled when returning to the rectory after his walk with Catherine on Wednesday. He then told me, at some considerable length, of events in 1632 that had occurred in the small village of Curbar, some two or three miles south-east of the parish. In that year, plague had visited the village; the ravages of which left desolation and depopulation in its wake. Whole families, including many members the Clarke and the Cooke households were almost totally lost to the plague; they were buried at various sites in and around the hamlet. Another family, the Cundys who lived at an isolated farm known as Grislow-fields, were also victims of the distemper. All five – Thomas Cundy; Ada, his wife; and Thomas, Olive and Nellie, their children – were buried below the gritstone crags of Curbar Edge. But, although clearly anxious to return to his dear wife's bedside, there was a constraint which somehow compelled William to remain and complete his narrative. So now, with an agitated tone in his voice, he went on to relate that in the same village a certain Mrs Sheldon, after visiting a household stricken by the plague, left to return home together with her husband. Upon leaving the house, she turned and exclaimed, 'Oh! My dear, how sweet the air smells!' Looking directly at me, William then declared that these were almost the very words that Catherine had spoken on Wednesday evening. The coincidence had been too much for him to stomach because, shortly after arriving home, this said Mrs Sheldon took the distemper and died. At this point, William stopped abruptly and returned to Catherine's bedchamber. We did not see him again all day.

Because of Catherine's incapacity, I returned to Shepherd's Flatt, having heard that Sarah and Robert Morten had died earlier in the week. When the Revd Stanley paid his regular visit last night, he brought with him the sad news that Margaret Morten had also died of the plague, shortly after having delivered a baby boy with the assistance of her husband. Matthew Morten was fearful that his motherless baby was suffering from the plague. I saw that the baby was indeed in some considerable distress and, when I saw the telltale buboes, my worst fears were confirmed.

From the hand of Beth Hounsfeild:
Saturday 25 August 1666

After breakfast yesterday, when it became apparent that the fever had only little time left to run, William, having once again asked the Revd Stanley to visit Marshall Howe's home, returned to Catherine's bedside. It was all too apparent that he feared that her end was nigh. Before leaving the table he made reference to the fact that Joan, Marshall Howe's wife, and William, his son, were both showing early signs of having contracted the plague. Then, almost by way of an afterthought, he made further reference to his return to the rectory on Wednesday evening, declaring that, even with the terrible events which he had experienced on a daily basis for the past months, nothing could have prepared him adequately for the stark truth of Catherine's condition which, in his heart, he knew he had now encountered. On that evening, he had stood transfixed, by her bedside, in a state of utter despair and not knowing which way to turn.

We heard that baby Morten died during the day. There's only Matthew Morten together with his four cows and his faithful greyhound, Flash, now remaining at Shepherd's Flatt.

Early this morning, before Catherine was interred in the graveyard, we were called by one of the domestics to William's closet, where we found our distraught kinsman languishing in unquenchable grief, despair and total incredulity. Even though he'd administered every known remedy against the distemper with his own hand, his dear wife had still been pitilessly snatched from him. William, in a complete state of shock, was too overcome to utter any words whatsoever; instead, he sat on the side of the bed, continually shaking his head in disbelief. Edward and I were told later that he had been found lying by the side of Catherine's decaying body, tears falling down his face as he desperately tried to face the reality of events. He had been persuaded to leave, whilst Catherine's body was prepared for burial, and as he had left her chamber he had been heard to cry, 'Farewell! Farewell, all happy days!'

Before the day ended I went to William's study, knowing that, in all probability, I would find him there. He was deep in prayer and, when he had assembled his thoughts, we talked of Catherine. William, totally grief-stricken, outpoured all of his deepest concerns, doubts and misgivings, as if wishing to expunge all the bitter events which had befallen him and filled the last three wearisome days. Perhaps the emotion that is uppermost in his mind is that of guilt; he blames himself for not insisting that Catherine vacated the parish when the children left in June. He also told me of Catherine's concerns for himself. Some weeks ago, when she saw a green ichor issuing from a wound on his leg, Catherine had been convinced that he too had been taken with the distemper. During the following days she had bathed and dressed the wound, giving no thought to her own well-being, even though the wasting consumption, which was still with her, rendered her very delicate. William said that, when he could face writing to George and Elizabeth in order to break the sad tidings to them, he would tell of the brave and courageous woman that their mother and his dear wife had been. His mind was awry – his sentences were disjointed, ranging through various aspects of Catherine's short life, her even shorter illness, and her deep and enduring love for himself and their dear children. He reflected on his entreaty for her to drink of the cordial, which she was only able to attempt for the sake of their dear children. He then acknowledged that, because her natural strength was impaired due to the consumption, her ability to struggle with the disease was thus reduced. On the first day of her illness, she had implored him not to come too close to her for fear of him too receiving harm and then, when given to contrition, repeated on a number of occasions, 'One drop of my Saviour's blood to save my soul!'

Before her soul departed they had prayed together, ending with prayers for the sick from the Common Prayer Book. Catherine had given all the correct responses and 'Amens'. Finally, they turned to *The Whole Duty of Man* but, at this point, she gave little response to William, whereupon he asked, 'My dear, dost thou mind?' She had answered yes; this was the last word that she spoke.

Before our time ended, we recited the words of the *Nunc Dimittis* together:

Lord, now lettest thou thy servant depart in peace: according to thy word.
For mine eyes have seen: thy salvation;
Which thou hast prepared: before the face of all people;
To be a light to lighten the Gentiles: and to be the glory of they people Israel.
Glory be to the father, and to the Son: and to the Holy Ghost;
As it was in the beginning, is now, and ever shall be: world without end.
Amen.

From the hand of Beth Hounsfeild:
Thursday 30 August 1666

I cannot begin to relate the terrible events that are happening in this
village, which Catherine once described as being, God-forsaken; and
I am now minded to share her assertion. This month has been without
parallel and almost beyond belief. I fail to comprehend how William is
continuing with his ministry around the village, following the death of his
beloved wife just less than one week ago. But so much has happened since
that dreadful time. On the very same day as Catherine's death, Samuel
Chapman and Anne Fryth died and since then William has recorded the
deaths of Joan Howe – Marshall Howe's wife – Thomas Ashemore and
Thomas Wood; and today he has informed me of the passing of William
Howe, Marshall Howe's young son, Francis Wilson, Katherine Talbott and
baby Mary Abell, who was just six months old. Following the death of her
mother, Elizabeth, it was not possible to get a wet nurse for the baby, so
Christopher Abell has endured a torrid time during these last months.

I believe that William has recorded no less than seventy-seven deaths
this month, including that of his dear wife.

Extract from the Journal of the Revd William Mompesson:
Friday 31 August 1666

The Revd Stanley and I made two visits this morning. First we went to the
home of the Wilsons, where two of their family have died recently. From
there we went to visit their neighbours who are caring for one-year-old
Robert Trickett. His parents, John and Anne Trickett, both died on the
same day earlier in the month and now the young child himself looks to be
in the final throes of the plague.

When I returned to the now deserted rectory at eventide, I resolved
to write to my dear hearts, George and Elizabeth. I am conscious of
the procrastination and lethargy of which I have been guilty in failing
to address this duty, this painful duty. Since the death of my dear wife,
Catherine, almost a week ago now, time has ceased to be and yet, in other
respects, time itself has hung so heavily on my soul.

After dinner I sat in my study and thought for many minutes before
finally committing my deepest and innermost thoughts to paper. My letter
is as follows:

To my dear children, George and Elizabeth Mompesson, these present with my blessing.

Eyam, 31 August 1666

DEAR HEARTS, – *This brings you the doleful news of your dear mother's death – the greatest loss which ever befel you! I am not only deprived of a kind and loving comfort, but you also is bereaved of the most indulgent mother that ever dear children had. But we must comfort ourselves in God with this consideration, that the loss is only ours, and that what is our sorrow is her gain. The consideration of her joys, which I do assure myself are unutterable, should refresh our drooping spirits.*

My dear hearts, your blessed mother lived a most holy life, and made a most comfortable and happy end, and is now invested with a crown of righteousness. I think it may be useful to you to have a narrative of your dear mother's virtues, that the knowledge thereof may teach you to imitate her excellent qualities. In the first place, let me recommend to you her piety and devotion, which were according to the exact principles of the Church of England. In the next place, I can assure you, she was composed of modesty and humility, which virtues did possess her dear soul in a most extraordinary manner. Her discourse was ever grave and meek, yet pleasant withal; a vaunting, immodest word was never heard to come from her mouth. Again, I can set out in her two other virtues i.e. charity and frugality. She never valued anything she had, when the necessities of a poor neighbour required it; but had a bountiful heart to all indigent and distressed persons. And, again, she was never lavish, but commendably frugal. She never liked tattling women, and abhorred the custom of going from house to house, thus wastefully spending precious time. She was ever busied in useful work, yet, though prudent, she was affable and kind. She avoided those whose company could not benefit her, and would not unbosom her to such, still she dismissed them with civility. I could tell you of her many other excellent virtues. I do believe, my dear hearts, upon sufficient grounds that she was the kindest wife in the world, and think, from my soul, that she loved me ten times better than herself; for she not only resisted my entreaties that she would fly with you, dear children, from this place of death; but some few days before it pleased God to visit my house, she perceived a green matter to come from the issue in my leg, which she fancied a symptom that the distemper had found vent that way, whence she assured herself that I was past the malignity of the disorder, whereat she rejoiced exceedingly, not considering her own danger thereby. I think, however, that she was mistaken in the nature of the discharge she saw: certainly it was the salve that made it look so green; yet her rejoicing on that account was a strong testimony of her love to me: for I am clear that she cared not (if I were safe) though her own dear self was in ever so much pain and jeopardy.

Further, I can assure you, my sweet babes, that her love to you was little inferior than to me; since why should she so ardently desire my continuance in this world of sorrows, but that you might have the protection and comfort of my life? You little imagine with what delight she talked of you both, and the pains she took when you sucked the milk from her breasts. She gave strong testimony of her love for you when she lay on her death-bed. A few hours before she expired I wished her to take some cordials which she told me plainly she could not take. I entreated she would attempt for your dear sakes. At the mention of your names, she with difficulty lifted up her head and took them; which was to let me understand that whilst she had any strength left she would embrace any opportunity she had of testifying her affection to you.

Now I will give you an exact account of the manner of her death. For some time she had shown symptoms of a consumption, and was wasted thereby. Being surrounded by infected families, she doubtless got the infection from them; and her natural strength being impaired, she could not struggle with the disease, which made her illness so very short. She showed much contrition for the errors of her past life, and often cried out, 'One drop of my Saviour's blood to save my soul!' At the beginning of her sickness she entreated me not to come near her, lest I should receive harm thereby; but, thank God, I did not desert her, but stood to my resolution not to leave her in sickness, who had been so tender a nurse to me in her health. Blessed be God, that He enabled me to be so helpful and consoling to her, for which she was not a little thankful. During her illness she was not disturbed by worldly business – she only minded making her calling and election sure; and she asked pardon of her maid for having sometimes given her an angry word. I gave her some sweating antidotes, which rather inflamed her more, whereupon her dear head was distempered, which put her upon many incoherencies. I was troubled thereat, and propounded to her questions in divinity; as by whom and on what account she expected salvation, and what assurances she had of the certainty thereof. Though in all other things she talked at random, yet to these religious questions she gave me as rational answers as could be desired. And at these times I bade her repeat after me certain prayers and ejaculations, which she did with great devotion, – it gave me comfort that God was so gracious to her.

A little before her dear soul departed (I was gone to bed) she sent for me to pray with her. I got up and went to her, and asked her how she did. The answer was, that she was looking when the good hour should come.

Thereupon I prayed, and she made her responses from the Common Prayer Book, as perfectly as in her health, and an 'Amen' to every pathetic expression. When we had ended the prayers for the sick, we used those from the Whole duty of Man! and when I heard her say nothing, I said, 'My dear, dost thou mind?' She answered, 'Yes,' and it was the last word she spoke.

My dear babes, the reading of this account will cause many a salt tear to spring from your eyes; yet let this comfort you, – your mother is a saint in heaven. I could have told you of many more of your dear mother's excellent virtues; but I hope that you will not in the least question my testimony, if in a few words I tell you that she was pious and upright in her demeanour and conversation.

Now to that blessed God, who bestowed upon her all those graces be ascribed all honour, glory and dominion, the just tribute of all created beings, for evermore. – Amen!

William Mompesson

Upon finishing the letter, I went to bed with a heavy heart, but yet rejoicing in the knowledge that my dear hearts now know of the death of their dear mother, and that my dear wife is together with her Saviour. I recited again the Jubilate Deo, the words of which give me continuing hope and belief in this time of great darkness.

From the hand of Beth Hounsfeild:
Friday 31 August 1666

William and the Revd Stanley went to visit the Wilson family this morning, where Francis had died yesterday; his wife, Anne, having died just two weeks ago. The Wilson offspring, Sarah, Ellin, Rowland and Elizabeth are still alive, but Sarah, the eldest, is now in need medication as it appears that she too has the distemper. Edward and I have pleaded with William to leave the parish and rejoin his dear children before he succumbs to the plague and leaves them orphans, but he holds to the belief that he has been given a calling from God, and that he must keep on ministering to the sick and dying.

Today was the first day that I had left the rectory since the passing of my dear cousin, Catherine. I walked out of the village in the general direction of Riley, intent on visiting Elizabeth Hancock. The wild countryside on either side of the now overgrown path was beginning to turn a deep hue of purple, as the heather and bell heather started to come into flower; heather had always been one of Catherine's favourites, ever since early childhood but, alas, no longer.

My visit to Riley was occasioned by a rumour that the Revd Stanley had heard in the village yesterday. Apparently, when Robert and Ruth Talbot, the only remaining members of the Talbot family had died towards the end of July, their one-year-old baby, Catharine, had been left on her own in the family home. Having buried all of her own family just days after the Talbots died, Elizabeth Hancock, as an act of neighbourliness, has been caring for the baby since that time. But, the baby too died yesterday, leaving Elizabeth distraught and heartbroken. When I arrived at the Hancock home, I found it to be completely deserted. I was thus inclined to agree with the commonly held view that Elizabeth had fled at first light and gone to live in Sheffield with her one surviving son, Joseph, who is bound as an apprentice in the cutlery trade at Alsop-Fields.

From the hand of Beth Hounsfeild:
Saturday 1 September 1666

In the normal course of events, not that anything during the last few months could be remotely considered as being normal, I was capable of keeping control of my innermost feelings, but today I was completely overwhelmed with an intense feeling of desolation, isolation and profound despondency. William and Edward had departed when the Revd Stanley had called sometime after breakfast. I remained seated at the dining table, now completely alone since my dearest cousin Catherine had succumbed to that dreadful pestilence. I was aware that William had written to George and Elizabeth, following dinner last night, and I grieved concerning the news which would surely reach them during the next days. I sat, gazing into the lambent flames in the fire, longing to be with those dear children and longing, even more, that Catherine could once again grace our company. I could hear the magpies and jays on the lawn outside, fighting over scraps of fat as usual, completely oblivious of the devastation within. The heaviness within my heart became too much to bear as I felt tears inexorably forming and rolling down my cheeks. I sat weeping, without caring or attempting to conceal my anguish, for some considerable time. But, during its passage, I was informed that Marshall Howe had called, wanting to speak with William. I met him and confirmed that neither William nor the Revd Stanley could be contacted until later in the day, as they were both engaged in parochial duties. As we talked he demonstrated a degree of compassion which, hitherto, I had not witnessed; extending his condolences for our sad loss. He went on to say that he too had recently lost his own dear wife and also his only son, William. Up until that point I had assumed, wrongly, that he was wishing to see William in connection with his duties as sextant, but this was not the case. Noticing that I'd been weeping, he inquired as to how I was coping and how William was facing his grievous loss. It soon became obvious that he was in no rush to depart, and was desirous of telling of the tragic events surrounding the death of his wife. Guilt-ridden, he told of how his wife had for many days past been imploring him to desist from his ghoulish, if profitable, activities; but Howe had opened a deaf ear to her pleas. It had now been almost two months since he had been engaged in this vulgar avocation, considering himself to be immune and thus invulnerable to the pest; but, when returning home on Sunday, he found that Joan had now been taken by the pestilence. It was only then that he first entertained the notion that he might have, unwittingly, been the means whereby the disease had been brought across his own threshold and that although he may have immunity from the plague, his wife and son might not have the same safeguard, never having suffered from the ravages of the disease. This single and simple thought brought sorrow to the callous heart of Marshall Howe.

Describing the days of her suffering, Howe recounted when the terrible telltale symptom appeared on her bosom, stating that, having witnessed similar virulent attacks, it was all too clear to him that her hold on life would rapidly evaporate and that she would soon be joining the ranks of his pastor's wife. Although she fought bravely throughout the period of the fever, she ultimately lost her futile battle; breathing her last on the morning of the twenty-seventh.

After committing his wife to her final resting place, in a carefully prepared grave, he returned home totally dejected where further grief befell him. Entering the house, a charnel odour rose from the room where William lay stricken with the disease. Being similar in stature and temperament to his father, he would not submit to the pestilence, but fought this unwanted visitor for three long days and nights; he died on Thursday, just three days after his mother. Marshall Howe was now alone, save for the spoils of his precarious avocation. He reopened the trench which was his wife's grave and then, with dignity and circumspection, emptied in his son's now putrefying and decaying body to be alongside that of his mother. There was an irony that Marshall Howe and William should both suffer in the same way at the unforgiving hand of Fate, in that both of the wives of these two very different men had been taken by the pestilence.

I have to own that, when talking with Marshall Howe, I was more than pleasantly surprised when he demonstrated an aspect of his character which, previously, was either absent or, being more charitable, had lain dormant. Until the death of his wife, he had always approached his unenviable avocation in a completely detached, even disdainful manner. But now, grieving himself, he seemed to be able to appreciate that when death visited, grief had to be endured by those who were left behind. And, judging from this enlightenment and apparent contrition, I became conscious that, in future, he would be approaching his task of interment with considerably more compassion and dignified demeanour than hitherto.

Before taking his leave, Howe remarked that there had only been three days in the last month when villagers hadn't died; an awful total of seventy-seven deaths in one month had consumed the village. It was clear that his work would continue for some time to come.

Extract from the Journal of the Revd William Mompesson:
Saturday 1 September 1666

The Revd Stanley called at the rectory shortly after breakfast this morning. After a time of prayer and contemplation, we left to return to West End Cottage, home of the Wilson family, in the company of the Revd Edward Hounsfeild, Beth's husband. On our arrival, we were asked to visit the home of their relative, Katherine Wilson; her husband, John, was thought to be suffering from the ravages of the plague. Like so many other close families in the parish, the Wilsons are now suffering untold anguish and sorrow, as the plague steadily and remorselessly casts its dark shadow over their homes.

I left my brothers to journey on to Eyam Moor where I had arranged to meet with another fellow priest, my friend, the Revd John Walker, Vicar of Hathersage. After having to bear the tragic loss of my dear wife, I felt compelled to contemplate the inevitable outcome of these grief-stricken times. Accordingly, during these last careworn days, I have made my will and appointed my executors, in the sure and certain belief that my time here, serving the Almighty God, is nearing its end. It now only remained for me to write to my patron, Sir George Savile, and explain the reasoning behind my resolve. In deference to him, and in the hope of reducing the risk of spreading the contamination from the seeds of the plague, I dictated the letter to the Revd John Walker.

The letter reads as follows:

To my friend and patron, Sir George Savile: –

Eyam, 1 September 1666

Honoured and dear Sir,
This is the saddest news that ever my pen could write. The destroying Angel having taken up his quarters within my habitation, my dearest wife is gone to her eternal rest, and is invested with a crown of righteousness, having made a happy end. Indeed had she loved herself as well as me, she had fled from the pit of destruction with the sweet babes, and might have prolonged

EYAM

Above left: 1. The Saxon Cross in the churchyard at Eyam.

Above right: 2. The Parish Church of Saint Lawrence. In the Revd Mompesson's time, the church's patron saint was Saint Helen.

Below: 3. The Miners Arms – still a popular venue in Eyam.

Above: **4.** Plague Cottage, where George Viccars died on 7 September 1665 – the first plague victim.

Left: **5.** The Hawksworth family home.

Above: **6.** Rose Cottage, where nine members of the Thorpe family died from the plague.

Right: **7.** Bagshaw House – home of Emmott Syddall.

8. The Royal Oak, built in 1587 and originally called the Heart of Oak.

9. The Boundary Stone.

Above: **10.** Mompesson's Well.

Right: **11.** Hollins House, home of Humphrey and Anne Merrill.

Left: 12. West End Cottage, home of the Wilson family.

Below: 13. The tomb of Catherine Mompesson.

BAKEWELL

14. The original fords across the river were replaced by bridges. The magnificent five-arch bridge is over 800 years old and still carries traffic into the town.

15. The Packhorse Bridge has been used by traders coming from the direction of Monyash since 1664. They thus avoided paying the taxes imposed if entering in the centre of the town.

16. The parish church of All Saints is a Grade I listed building. A church was founded on this site in 920.

17. Behind the Old Town Hall are the Bakewell Almshouses. The almshouses were founded 'so that we can give charitable disposition towards the relief of poor people inhabiting the town of Bakewell'.

Hope

Right: **18.** The parish church of St Peter is the only church in North Derbyshire mentioned in the Domesday Book.

Below: **19.** The Cheshire Cheese Inn. Traders from Cheshire paid for their lodging in rounds of Cheshire cheese!

TIDESWELL

20. The magnificent fourteenth-century parish church of St John the Baptist, known as 'The Cathedral of The Peak'.

WALK TO BOUNDARY STONE

21. The family butcher's of George Siddall & Daughters – The Causeway, Eyam.

22. The Lydgate Graves, where father and daughter George and Mary Darby were buried.

23. The cottages.

Above: **24.** Footpath to the Boundary Stone.

Left: **25.** Part of the narrow footpath on the way to the Boundary Stone.

26. Open land where some of the pest houses were built.

27. Boundary Stone detail – showing holes where coins were placed in exchange for food and medicines.

28. The village stocks were first installed by the Barmote Court and were for the punishment of lead-miners who were found guilty of infringing its laws.

29. Eyam View Farm.

30. Shepherd's Flatt farm, where the Mortens and Kempes lived – and died!

31. The village duck pond, Foolow, with the church of Saint Hugh's in the background.

32. Along Bradshaw Lane, looking towards Eyam Edge after leaving the hamlet of Foolow.

33. The Barrel Inn is said to be the highest pub in the county of Derbyshire.

her days; but she was resolved to die a martyr to my interests. My drooping spirits are much refreshed with her joys, which I think are unutterable.

Sir, this paper is to bid you a hearty farewell for ever, and to bring you my humble thanks for all your noble favours; and I hope you will believe a dying man, I have as much love as honour for you, and I will bend my feeble knees to the God of Heaven, that you, my dear lady, and your children, may be blessed with external and eternal happiness, and that the same blessing may fall upon Lady Sunderland and her relations.

Dear Sir, let your dying Chaplain recommend this truth to you and your family, that no happiness or solid comfort can be found in this vale of tears, like living a pious life; and pray ever remember this rule, never do anything upon which you dare not first ask the blessing of God upon the success thereof.

Sir, I have made bold in my will with your name for executor, and I hope you will not take it ill. I have joined two others with you, who will take from you the trouble. Your favourable aspect, will I know, be a great comfort to my distressed orphans. I am not desirous that they should be great, but good; and my next request is that they be brought up in the fear and admonition of the Lord.

Sir, I thank God I am contented to shake hands with all the world; and have many comfortable assurances that God will accept me through His Son. I find the goodness of God greater than I ever thought or imagined; and I wish from my soul that it were not so much abused contemned. I desire, Sir, that you will be pleased to make choice of a humble, pious man, to succeed me in my parsonage; and could I see your face before my departure hence, I would inform you in what manner I think he may live comfortable amongst his people, which would be some satisfaction to me before I die.

Dear Sir, I beg the prayers of all about you that I may not be daunted at the powers of hell; and that I may have dying graces; with tears I beg that when you are praying for fatherless orphans, you will remember my two pretty babes. Sir pardon the rude style of this paper, and if my head be discomposed you cannot wonder at mee, however be pleased to believe that I am.

Dear Sir,
Your most obliged, most affectionate and
gratefull servant,
William Mompesson

Having dictated the letter, I bade farewell to my brother-in-Christ and made my way back to the rectory. Upon my return I was told that Margaret Frith had called to inform me that her sister, Elizabeth, just ten years old, had died today and that her brother, Henry, now appeared to be suffering from the plague. Their father, Francis Frith, our churchwarden, had died early in August, and their dear mother, Elizabeth, had been buried just five days before my own dear wife. Another of the Friths' children, twelve-year-old Anne, had also died on the same day as my dear wife.

I prayed to the Almighty, as I pray every day and every hour, for deliverance from this wretched pestilence.

Extract from the Journal of the Revd William Mompesson:
Sunday 2 September 1666

My friend and brother-in-Christ, the Revd John Walker, Vicar of Hathersage, called to see me following Divine Worship this morning. Although we'd met on Eyam Moor only yesterday, when I'd dictated to him my letter to Sir George Saville, he felt obliged to call today in order to inform me of a postscript to the letter which, under the circumstances, he deemed to be necessary. It was his view, and I concurred fully with his reasoning, that a postscript was necessary in order to reassure Sir George that he was in no danger of infection.

He left me a copy of the postscript, which reads as follows:

Honoured Sir,

Mr Mompesson did not write this, but dictated it to mee yesterday upon Eyam Moore, & desires you would be pleased to consider Mr Wright, he having a very hard bargain of the Lott & Cope by reason of the infection, & sayes he would have bin silent in it, had he not mocioned Mr Wright to it. A boy came from him this day, & told mee an imperfect story that he desired Mr Gardner to send him some Cordiall spirits.

(Blessed be God) He is yet in good health. Soe rests
Your Worship's humble servant
John: Walker Vic.
Hathersage. September 2, 1666

From the hand of Beth Hounsfeild:
Tuesday 4 September 1666

I had only met Mary Darby once before and that was on the day, sometime in early July, when she had asked William to take the Last Will and Testament of her dear husband George Darby. He had died that very day. And now she had come to the rectory from their home at Lydgate to convey some more distressing news. Since her father's death, their lovely young daughter, also called Mary, had taken to the habit of wandering out amongst the fields around their home and picking flowers which she then placed on his grave. Only yesterday she had been out, smiling and singing and gathering a posy when she was suddenly seized by the pestilence. She died early this morning, and has now been laid to her final resting place, next to her father, by Marshall Howe. Mary was inconsolable, having lost both her husband and younger daughter within the space of two short months.

Mary said that she would not visit her married daughter, Elizabeth, who also lives in the parish, for fear of spreading the contagion to her one-year-old granddaughter, Anne.

From the hand of Beth Hounsfeild:
Sunday 9 September 1666

Only this morning, following Divine Worship, did I hear of the terrible events which have surrounded the family of our late churchwarden, Francis Frith, who died early last month. Apparently, having heard that his sister, who lived over at Lydgate, was suffering from the ravages of the plague, Francis took himself over to visit her as she lay dying. However, upon reaching the stricken house, he found that the plague had already claimed its victim and that his sister had been buried by Marshall Howe and most of the remaining contents of the home had been removed by the said Howe. But, worse was to come; having returned home to tell his wife and family of the sad events, he too found that he had contracted the disease. Over the course of the next days and weeks, he and most of his family fell victim to the distemper; one of his sons, George, having died just two days ago.

From the hand of Beth Hounsfeild:
Tuesday 11 September 1666

Having accompanied Catherine to the home of Humphrey and Anne Merrill, on several occasions during the last few agonising months, it was with a heavy heart that I made my visit this morning. William, who is still grief-stricken at the passing of his dear wife, my cousin Catherine, informed me of the death of Humphrey Merrill on Sunday last. Because of his profession as an apothecary, Humphrey was, on a daily basis, encountering people exhibiting signs and symptoms of the pestilence. Ultimately, he too has fallen victim to the plague, leaving Anne a widow. She was still finding it difficult coming to terms with the impact of his untimely death, even though they too had witnessed the carnage of the previous months.

During our conversation, she told me of the solution which their near-relative, Andrew Merrill, had adopted. Like many other people who had decamped from the village, Andrew had taken himself away immediately before Humphrey died and was now living in a hut which he had built on Eyam Moor. I knew that the Andrew's hut would be near to several others which had been built there during the last few weeks. I had also been told that John and Mary Coates had built a hut near to Riley and they, similarly to Andrew, would dwell there until the pestilence abated. Talking to Anne, it was truly amazing to learn of the number of huts which had been or were being built; she mentioned that some were even being built under the projecting rocks in the dale that leads up to Foundley. I made reference to the dwellings which had been built in Cussy Dell.

Before leaving that sad house, Anne said that Andrew's hut was high up on the moors from where he could overlook the village. She also said that he had taken with him one of his favourite cockerels to be his sole companion.

Extract from the Journal of the Revd William Mompesson:
Wednesday 19 September 1666

Beth had paid a visit to Hollins House last week, shortly after the death of Humphrey Merrill. It was now my sad duty to assist widow Merrill in obtaining probate – a task which for which, Beth assures me, she is ill-equipped. Although summer is not yet over and the weather is still very warm, there was a blazing fire roaring up the chimney. We sat talking for some time at the kitchen table before starting to make an assessment of the extent of Humphrey's assets. I considered that his sheep would be worth about £9 when taken to market, and I estimated that his horses would have a market value of £2 10s. I thought that his other stock, two bullocks, five cows and two stirks would fetch, perhaps, £14 16s 8d. In total, the farm stock and domestic goods were valued at £40 3s 6d.

During our talk I also asked about other close relatives, as Humphrey and Anne Merrill did not have any children living at home. Anne told me that their close relative, Andrew Merrill had, during the previous week, taken himself to a hut which he had built on Eyam Moor, overlooking the village. He went, together with his cockerel who would be his sole companion, declaring that he would reside therein until the plague abated.

After meeting with the Revd Stanley, he said that he would pass the information to his brother John at Chesterfield who would arrange for probate.

From the hand of Beth Hounsfeild:
Friday 12 October 1666

Over dinner last night, William asked me if I would visit Widow Merrill this morning, as he'd heard that Andrew Merrill had unexpectedly returned to Hollins House. It is undoubtedly true that since William visited there towards the end of September, there has been a marked decrease in the number of deaths occurring in the village, perhaps because Autumn is coming upon us.

I was aware that Jonas Parsley had died sometime last week, but it came as a complete surprise to me, when speaking to the widow Merrill, to hear that Jonas Parsley's wife, Anne, had died yesterday; I'd been speaking to her after Divine Worship less than two weeks ago.

Andrew Merrill gave comfort by recounting that, from his vantage point high above the village, he could observe that the number of graves being added to in the fields below seemed to be increasing less rapidly than they had been previously. He then related to us an event of far more significance. Some three days ago, shortly after sunrise, his sole companion, the cockerel, ventured out of the hut and onto the surrounding heath; and then, after taking a cursory glance around, flapped its wings and flew to its former home at Hollins House – Merrill, being able to see this from where he stood. Sensing that this must be an omen, he nonetheless waited for two full days before venturing back into the village. Upon his return, he suggested that 'Noah knew when the dove went forth and returned not again that the waters had subsided, and that the face of the earth was dry'. I left with a joyous heart.

Later in the evening, when William was discussing parochial matters with the Revd Stanley in the study, I broached the subject with Edward as to the possibility of our returning to Dungeon. He reminded me that many people had died since September, including, amongst others, a number of members of the Morten family; the apprentice George Butterworth from Stoney Middleton; Anne Townend had died sometime in September and then, just a few days later her un-christened baby had also died, leaving her husband Francis to bring up their other three children, as best he could. Edward, rightly, cautioned me as to entertaining any hopes of an early return to Lancashire.

From the hand of Beth Hounsfeild:
Thursday 18 October 1666

On hearing that Elizabeth Daniel, formerly Elizabeth Syddall, had died yesterday, I visited her home this morning, together with the Revd Thomas Stanley. I was aware that her second husband, John Daniel, had died on 5 July, and was concerned for the well-being of her sole-surviving child, Joseph, who wouldn't reach three years of age until the turn of the month. When we arrived, we were assured that, although she had indeed died intestate, she had, on the day of her death, called in her close friend and neighbour, Rebecca Hawksworth, to whom she had given a solemn and verbal declaration. This statement, which was then testified in front of the Revd Stanley, affirmed that her estate was to be used for the upbringing of the child until he was old enough to inherit and manage the residue of the estate for himself and, until that time, he was to be raised in the care of her 'trusted friend' Mr Robert Thorpe. For his part, the Revd Stanley said that he would contact his brother, an attorney in Chesterfield, and have a Letter of Administration drawn up for the court.

CHAPTER SEVEN
THE BEGINNING OF THE END

Extract from the Journal of the Revd William Mompesson:
Tuesday 23 October 1666

It has been almost two weeks now since Andrew Merrill returned to the village and, since that time, there have only been another seven reported deaths, and those were mainly in the outlying hamlet of Bretton. I have also noticed that some of the children of the parish are now beginning to return, after their enforced absence. I will not, however, countenance my two dear babes returning, until such time as the pestilence has departed without a trace. But, as life is slowly returning to the village, so it would appear, my more immediate concern is to ensure that we remove as many of the infested articles remaining in the village as possible. I discussed my proposals with the Revd Stanley and we agreed that I would make an announcement following Sunday's service of Divine Worship. My proposal is that all infected and unnecessary items of clothing, bedding and furniture should be burnt. Assuming that my parishioners agree to this final act of self-sacrifice, I will personally supervise the burnings.

From the hand of Beth Hounsfeild:
Wednesday 24 October 1666

At dinner this evening, William talked to Edward, and myself, and told of his plans for burning unnecessary clothing, bedding and other items of furniture which might be infected; as he said, it appears that the pestilence is now departing the parish and, coupled with that, some of the village children are beginning to return to the homes of their parents. I know that William considers that the seven deaths that there have been in recent weeks have, in the main, been confined to the hamlet of Bretton, where Catherine and I had spent many happy hours together. I am aware that brothers Peter and Samuel Hall of Bretton died as recently as 13 October, as did Francis Morten's son, Joseph – Francis himself having died towards the end of September. His dear wife, Grace, followed him to the grave at the start of this month. Two more of their children, young Grace and Francis, have succumbed in the intervening period. It has also been reported that one of their servants, a fourteen-year-old girl called Anne Grundy, has also fallen victim.

Because of these recent deaths, I am concerned that William isn't making this move too precipitously. I voiced my concerns to Edward, but he thought that all would be well.

Extract from the Journal of the Revd William Mompesson:
Monday 5 November 1666

Following the service of Divine Worship yesterday, I made my announcement with regards to the burning of unnecessary items of infected clothing, bedding and furniture; exhorting members of my dwindling flock to make this final sacrifice, so as not to allow the pestilence to continue amongst us, especially now that some of the children of the village are returning to their parental homes.

I spent much of today burning clothes, bedding and furniture at various locations in the parish, together with my brothers-in-Christ, the Revds Stanley and Hounsfeild, who, throughout the prolonged period of this terrible pestilence, have been a constant source of support and succour. I envisage that many more days will be taken up with this necessary duty. The Revd Stanley said that he would venture out to some of the pest-houses and burn whatever he deemed to be necessary. We will then have to set about the task of fumigating and then reconditioning all of the infected households, as I believe has been the practice in other towns which have had similar visitations.

From the hand of Beth Hounsfeild:
Tuesday 6 November 1666

Following Edward's advice, I voiced my concerns to William about his precipitous action with regards to the burnings, but he is firmly of the opinion that the pestilence has finally vacated the village. He has even suggested to Edward and the Revd Stanley that, following the last of the burnings, they should hold a service of thanksgiving at Cucklett Church.

This afternoon, when walking through the village near to Lydgate, I encountered a forlorn Rowland Torre coming along the footpath from Stoney Middleton. He'd walked past the boundary stone – knowing, from the burnings which have already started, that the pestilence has now departed. He had been betrothed to Emmott Syddall, and they were to have been married at Wakestide but, in April, Emmott was taken by the plague. As he had been entreated by Emmott not to visit their secret meeting place in the Delph, Rowland was still unsure as to what fate had befallen his betrothed. However, immediately before I met him, a tactless youth from the village had shouted to him, 'Ah! Rowland, thy Emmott's dead and buried in Cussy Dell.' It was confirmation, if any were necessary, and put an end to any faint hope that he may have been harboured. Hardly able to look at me, his grief was all too apparent; he turned and walked into a dark unknown.

Extract from the Journal of the Revd William Mompesson:
Tuesday 20 November 1666

I have, as of late, deliberately refrained from committing any events in the parish to this journal, fearing, as has happened in the past, that my deliberations may be completely misguided, misplaced or hold out false hope; but it now appears certain that this dreadful pestilence has taken its leave of the village, for which I truly give thanks to our Redeemer, the Lord Jesus Christ.

William Morten, the eldest of Francis and Grace Morten's family, died on 28 October; he was the last surviving member of the Morten family of Shepherd's Flatt. There had not then been another death in the parish until 1 November, when Abraham Morten also of Shepherd's Flatt, Bretton, died; he, together with his younger brother Godfrey, lived with their sister, Mary. From meetings that I have since had, with the Revd Stanley and also from conversations with Beth and Edward, I am not aware of any parishioner now suffering from the plague, so I have reason to believe that it might, finally, have departed.

I wrote the following letter to my esteemed uncle.

Dear Sir,

I suppose this letter will seem to you no less than a miracle, that my
habitation is inter vivos. I have got these lines transcribed by a friend,
being loth to affright you with a letter from my hands. You are sensible
of my state, the loss of the kindest wife in the world, whose life was
amiable, and end most comfortable. She was in an excellent posture
when death came, which fills me with assurance that she is now invested
with a crown of righteousness. I find this maxim verified by too sad
experience: Bonum magis carendo quam fruendo cernitur. Had I been as
thankful as my condition did deserve, I might have had my dearest dear
in my bosom. But now farewell all happy days, and God grant that I may
repent my sad ingratitude!

The condition of the place has been so sad, that I persuade myself that
it did exceed all history and example. Our town has become a Golgotha,
the place of a skull: and had there not been a small remnant left, we
had been as Sodom, and like to Gomorrah. My ears never heard such
doleful lamentations – my nose never smelled such horrid smells, and my
eyes never beheld such ghastly spectacles. There have been 76 families
visited within my parish, out of which 259 persons died. Now (blessed
be God) all our fears are over, for none have died of the plague since the
eleventh of October, and the pest houses have been long empty. I intend
(God willing) to spend this week in seeing all woollen clothes fumed
and purified, as well for the satisfaction as for the safety of the country.
Here have been such burning of goods that the like, I think, was never
known. For my part, I have scarcely apparel to shelter my body, having
wasted more than I needed merely for example. During this dreadful
visitation, I have not had the least symptom of disease, nor had I ever
better health. My man had the distemper, and upon the appearance of a
tumour I gave him some chemical antidotes, which operated, and after
the rising broke, he was very well. My maid continued in health, which
was a blessing; for had she quailed, I should have been ill set to have
washed and gotten my provisions. I know I have had your prayers; and I
conclude that the prayers of good people have rescued me from the jaws
of death. Certainly I had been in the dust had not Omnipotence itself
been conquered by holy violence.

I have largely tasted of the goodness of the Creator, and the grim looks
of death did never yet affright me. I always had a firm faith that my
babes would do well, which made me willing to shake hands with the
unkind, forward world; yet I shall esteem it a mercy if I am frustrated

in the hopes I had of a translation to a better place, and God grant that
with patience I may wait for my change, and that I may make a right use
of His mercies; as the one has been tart, so the other hath been sweet and
comfortable.

I perceive by a letter from Mr Newby, of your concern for my welfare.
I make no question but I have your unfeigned love and affection. I assure
you that during my troubles you have had a great deal of room in my
thoughts. Be pleased, dear Sir, to accept the presentments of my kind
respects, and impart them to your good wife and all my dear relations.
I can assure you that a line from your hand will be welcome to your
sorrowful and affectionate nephew.

William Mompesson

Having written the above letter, I journeyed to Stoney Middleton, where
I had it transcribed; being loath to affright Mr John Beilby with a paper
from my hands. When, at the beginning of September, I had written to
my friend and patron, Sir George Savile, informing him of the death of
my dear wife, I had, in deference to him, dictated the letter in the hope of
reducing the risk of spreading the seeds of the plague.

From the hand of Beth Hounsfeild:
Saturday 24 November 1666

Following our repast last evening, and knowing that we were starting on
our journey back to Speke on Monday, William thought that we may wish
to visit some of the places which had been of significance to us during the
last painful months.

Immediately after breaking our fast this morning, Edward and I set
off on what was to be a last walk around the village. There were many
mixed emotions in my mind as we left the rectory and walked over to
the churchyard; the very place where William had buried Catherine on
25 August. I knew from my many times spent in accompanying her, that
Catherine had worked tirelessly during the period of the plague, but now
had earned her reward in heaven. William had told us some time ago that
he had commissioned a more fitting memorial to mark his dear wife's final
resting place. It would serve as a tribute to his dear wife; to her resolute
and steadfast endeavours during the time of the distemper. After spending
some time in thoughtful meditation we walked along and, before entering
into the parish church, we read the inscription on the headstone of young
Abell Rowland – yet another victim of the plague, who was interred on

15 January last. His father, Thomas, had died just one month later. As we walked into the church, Edward described the Norman pillars which are set on Saxon bases and stand between the nave and the north aisle, although Catherine had described them to me in some detail shortly after we had arrived in the parish, but perhaps Edward wasn't to know that. We then went over to the south aisle to study the glass window, but also took time to look at the windows in both the chancel and the north aisle; this window is enriched with some very ancient glass.

After leaving the churchyard we found ourselves at the group of cottages which, since last year, have colloquially become known as the plague cottages. It was here, so many months ago now, that George Viccars became the first victim of this terrible pestilence. Perhaps the adjoining cottages proved to be an even more distressing sight, because it was here, in the first cottage, that Peter Hawksworth became the third victim of the plague. Many members of the Hawksworth family have died during the last months. In Rose Cottage, next to the cottage where Viccars was living, nine members of the Thorpe family died from the plague. I well recall that Catherine visited the home at the beginning of October last year when Elizabeth Thorpe had died, only five days after her husband, Thomas – the fourth victim claimed by the distemper. Directly across the road from the plague cottages we could see Bagshaw House; the pestilence having paid an early visit here. This was the home of the Syddalls, where Emmot Syddall died, together with her father, brother and four sisters during the plague. She died earlier in the year on the 29th of April. Her mother remarried four days before Emmott's death, but she herself died in October.

We didn't tarry here longer than necessary, but walked up past the market house, where all activity had ceased for another day. Edward commented that the nearby stocks are still redundant, and then observed that there hasn't been much call to punish recalcitrant lead-miners in the recent past. We were intending to walk through to Cucklett Delph, where William had held his services of Divine Worship during much of the time of the visitation of the plague, but a slight breeze was beginning to blow so we decided to walk on, making our way up the village in the direction of Town Head, passing the house which is still occupied by Francis and Margaret Blackwell – Margaret now having fully recovered. Even amidst all of the problems of the last months, it's still heartening to see that life is returning to the village, especially knowing that their parents and siblings had died at the height of the distemper. We passed the Royal Oak, a hostelry that William had pointed out to Edward although I don't believe that they ever entered the inn itself. We then turned up the lane and headed towards the place where Humphrey Merrill had been buried. I well recalled the number of times that Catherine and I walked to Humphrey Merrill's home, to speak with him and his dear wife, Anne, and also to exchange plague remedies for the sick and dying. But, alas, Humphrey Merrill had also succumbed to the pestilence in early September. After resting and reflecting there for some little while, we made our way back to the main road and continued towards Town Head.

We walked past one of the smithies which, judging from the activity around the anvil, now looked as though they were beginning to find work once again; shoeing horses, making plough shares for the farmers and other implements for the quarrymen and lead-miners. It's here that the Jumber Brook flows underground beneath Fiddler's Bridge. We came to Orchard Bank where, on one of our many walks around the village, Catherine had told me the area had become known as such because of nearby orchards which had been owned by the Stafford and Bradshaw families. Edward reminded me of the woman from this area who tried, unsuccessfully, to escape to Tideswell at the height of the plague.

We then walked to the junction with Tideswell Lane, where we saw the home of Marshall Howe, and I well remember the long conversation which I had with him at the rectory immediately following the deaths of his wife and only son, William. Since that time, I've heard that Howe has become a reformed character although, I believe, he still pursued his pitiful avocation until relatively recently.

When we arrived at Shepherd's Flatt, Edward suggested that we should perhaps walk as far as the hamlet of Foolow but, having walked this far, I was desirous to return to the village, as I particularly wanted to visit the boundary known as Mompesson's Well for one last time. We walked back to Hawks Hill where we turned and walked along the Edge until we arrived at the well. Catherine and I had walked to this spot on many occasions to take delivery of medicaments and other provisions. It was particularly poignant as we stood watching children, full of life, playing around the well which held so many tender memories for me.

We returned to the rectory, as it was now approaching our normal lunchtime hour. At lunch, William looked to be in a particularly contemplative mood. Whether he was contemplating the loss of his dear wife, and her exhortations to quit the village when the plague was in its early stages, or thinking of our imminent departure I cannot say; all I can record is that he was engrossed in his own, very deep, thoughts at that time. He agreed to join us on our walk to the boundary stone this afternoon. Leaving the rectory, we walked towards the Square where we saw the bullring. I'd first seen it at the time of the Wakes Festival last year, but of course, there had been no Wakes Festival this year. We then crossed from the Square, walked over to Lydgate and stopped at the graves where George Darby and his daughter, Mary, are buried in the former Parson's Field. When we arrived there we saw George Darby's wife, Mary, who was tending the graves. We talked for some while, before continuing on our way to the boundary stone, along the footpath leading to Stoney Middleton.

Our walk today, whilst evoking many memories, was nonetheless filled with too many painful reminders of the last, bitter and tragic months. We sat very quietly in the drawing room this evening, none of us wishing to speak, knowing full well where our thoughts lay. We prayed together before retiring for the night.

From the hand of Beth Hounsfeild
Monday 26 November 1666

After breaking our fast, we bade our farewells and set off on the long journey back to Speke.

Postscript

The last victim of the plague is reported as being Abraham Morten of Shepherd's Flatt, who died on 1 November 1666. By that time, not only had the Revd William Mompesson lost his dear wife Catherine to the plague but he was totally exhausted, both mentally and physically. In a letter to his uncle he wrote: 'My ears never heard such doleful lamentations. My nose never smelt such noisome smells, and my eyes never beheld such ghastly spectacles. There have been 76 families visited within my parish, out of which died 259 persons.' Mompesson continued his ministry in the parish of Eyam, helping to rebuild the broken community and its people. But the trials and tribulations of the last fourteen months had taken their toll on both Mompesson and the families in the parish. He was relieved of his appointment at Eyam. In 1669, some three years after the cessation of the plague and shortly before being remarried, William Mompesson was presented with the benefice of Eakring, near Newark, Nottinghamshire, by his friend and patron, Sir George Savile.

In 1670 William Mompesson remarried. His wife, Elizabeth Newby, was a relative of Sir George Savile.

Mompesson was not universally welcomed by his parishioners at Eakring, having come from the plague village of Eyam. He was precluded from entering both the parish church and vicarage; his parishioners being fearful that he might still be carrying the plague. However, it is known that both the church and parsonage house were in a very poor state of repair. It is believed Mompesson himself contributed much of the funds needed to render the parsonage house habitable. During the time in which the church and parsonage house were being refurbished, Mompesson and his wife were obliged to live in a house which she owned in nearby Rufford Park, which was on the Savile Estate.

William and Elizabeth Mompesson had four children, two daughters, Eliza and Jane, and two sons, both of whom died in infancy.

In 1676 Mompesson became a Prebendary Canon of Southwell. Some time later he became a Prebend of York. Grateful people wished to confer other honours upon him, including that of the Deanery of Lincoln, but Mompesson refused these, stating that he now desired a somewhat quieter life.

William Mompesson died on 7 March 1708, after having been rector of Eakring for thirty-eight years. He died in the seventieth year of his age. He is buried in Eakring Church.

Following the cessation of the plague, the Revd Thomas Stanley, similar to the Revd Mompesson, continued his work in the parish until his own health began to fail. He died on St Bartholomew's Day, 1670, the eighth anniversary of his deposition from his living at Eyam. He was buried in the village on 26 August, although the exact burial place is not known.

> He dy'd in 1670, fatisfy'd to the laft in the Caufe of Nonconformity, and rejoicing in his Sufferings on that Account.

In 1868/69, the north aisle of the church at Eyam was rebuilt to mark the bicentenary of the passing of the plague, and also the heroism of the rector, Revd William Mompesson, and a former incumbent of the parish, the Revd Thomas Stanley. The brass plaque affixed to the wall bears the inscription:

> This Memorial Aisle was erected by Voluntary Contributions obtained in 1866, to commemorate the Christian and Heroic virtues of the Revd W. Mompesson (rector), Catharine his Wife, and the Revd T. Stanley (late rector). When this place was visited by the Plague in 1665–6, they steadfastly continued to succour the afflicted and to minister amongst them the Truths and consolations of the Gospel of Jesus Christ. The rebuilding and enlarging of the Aisle led to the restoration of almost the entire Church, in 1868–9, at the cost of £2160.

There is now a memorial stone in the churchyard at Eyam dedicated to the memory of the Revd Thomas Stanley, even though he is not buried there.

Marshall Howe continued with his ghoulish, yet profitable, avocation until the end of the plague's visitation. But, after his wife died of the plague on 27 August 1666, followed by his only son, William, just three days later, he was a little more circumspect in his dealings with the dead. Howe remained a resident of the village for many years after the plague had departed and was laid to rest on 20 April 1698. However, his name lived on; for some generations after the plague, parents in Eyam would threaten to send for Marshall Howe if their children misbehaved.

Matthew Morten had lost his wife, Margaret, his children, Robert and Sarah, and his newly born son to the plague. Now alone, he lived, together with his four cows and his faithful greyhound, Flash, at Shepherd's Flatt. A little while after the plague had departed the village, Matthew was sitting outside the back door of his home, with his greyhound at his side. The dog, seeing a woman walking along the hillside above, ran to greet her. The explanation which Morten ascribed to the incident was that the dog had mistaken her for his former mistress. However, as an outcome of that chance meeting, a friendship was formed – which later resulted in marriage – between Morten and the lady who was Sarah Hawksworth. Her late husband, Peter Hawksworth, had been the third of the plague's victims.

DEATHS DURING THE PLAGUE

Accounts vary as to the exact number of deaths during the plague, as indeed do the spelling of some of the names. Some of the deaths were caused by factors other than the plague, some deaths occurred outside of the village and are not recorded as such; and other deaths are of un-baptised infants born during the plague and are sometimes not recorded as deaths due to the plague.

There is also some debate as to whether the dates recorded are of death or the burial of the deceased, as this fact is not noted in the records. There are also some deaths which do not have a specific date shown against them in the records.

September 1665

George Viccars	m	7th	Thomas Thorpe	m	26th
Edward Cooper	m	22nd	Sarah Syddall	f	30th
Peter Hawksworth	m	23rd	Mary Thorpe	f	30th

October 1665

Matthew Banes	m	1st	Martha Banes	f	17th
Elizabeth Thorpe	f	1st	Jonathan Ragge	m	18th
Margaret Banes	f	3rd	Humphrey Torre	m	19th
Mary Thorpe	f	3rd	Thomas Thorpe	m	19th
Sythe Torre	f	6th	Mary Banes	f	20th
William Thorpe	m	7th	Elizabeth Syddall	f	22nd
Richard Syddall	m	11th	Alice Ragge	f	23rd
William Torre	m	13th	Alice Syddall	f	24th
Amy Torre (his wife)	f	13th	George Ragge	m	26th
John Syddall	m	14th	Jonathan Cooper	m	28th
Ellen Syddall	f	15th	Humphrey Torre	m	30th
Humphrey Hawksworth	m	17th			

November 1665

Hugh Stubbs	m	1st	Ann Stubbs (his wife)	f	19th
Alice Taylor	f	3rd	Elizabeth Warrington	f	29th
Hannah Rowland	f	5th	Randoll Daniel	m	30th
John Stubbs	m	15th			

December 1665

Mary Rowland	f	1st	William Rowe	m	19th
Richard Coyle	m	2nd	Thomas Wilson	m	22nd
John Rowbottom	m	9th	William Rowbottom	m	24th
— Rowe (an infant)	m	14th	Anthony Blackwell	m	24th
Mary Rowe	f	15th			

January 1666

Robert Rowbottom	m	1st	Abel Rowland	m	15th
Samuel Rowbottom	m	1st	Isaac Wilson	m	28th

February 1666

Peter Morten, Bretton	m	4th	Alice Wilson	f	18th
Thomas Rowland	m	14th	Adam Hawksworth	m	18th
John Wilson	m	15th	Anthony Blackwell	m	21st
Deborah Wilson	f	17th	Elizabeth Abell	f	27th

March 1666

John Wilson, Jnr	m	1st	Mary Buxton, Foolow	f	Not recorded
John Talbot	m	4th	Anne Blackwell	f	22nd
John Wood	m	Not recorded	Alice Hawksworth	f	Not recorded

April 1666

Thomas Allen	m	6th	Samuel Hadfield	m	18th
Joan Blackwell	f	6th	Margaret Gregory	f	21st
Alice Thorpe	f	15th	— Allen (an infant)	m	28th
Edward Barnsley	m	16th	Emmott Syddall	f	29th
Margaret Blackwell	f	16th			

May 1666

Robert Thorpe	m	2nd	James Taylor	m	11th
William Thorpe	m	2nd	Ellen Charlesworth	f	24th

June 1666

Isaac Thornley	m	1st	Sarah Lowe	f	17th
Anne Thornley	f	12th	Mary Mellor	f	18th
Jonathan Thornley	m	12th	Jane Thornley	f	18th

Anthony Skidmore	m	12th	Anne Townsend	f	19th
Elizabeth Thornley	f	15th	Abel Archdale	m	20th
James Mower	m	15th	Edward Thornley	m	22nd
Edytha Mower	f	15th	Anne Skidmore	f	24th
Elizabeth Buxton	f	15th	Jane Townsend	f	25th
Mary Heald	f	16th	Emmott Heald	f	26th
Francis Thornley	m	17th	John Swann	m	29th
Mary Skidmore	f	17th			

July 1666

Elizabeth Heald	f	1st	Robert Whiteley, Snr	m	18th
William Lowe	m	2nd	Thomas Ashe	m	18th
Eleanor Lowe (his wife)	f	2nd	William Thornley	m	19th
Deborah Elliott	f	3rd	Francis Wood	m	22nd
George Darby	m	4th	Thomas Thorpe	m	22nd
Anne Coyle	f	5th	Robert Thorpe	m	22nd
Briget Talbot, Riley	f	5th	Robert Talbot	m	24th
Mary Talbot, Riley	f	5th	Joan Naylor	f	25th
John Daniel	m	5th	Thomas Healley	m	25th

Elizabeth Swann	f	6th	Richard Talbot	m	25th
Mary Thornley	f	6th	John Naylor	m	26th
John Townsend	m	7th	Joan Talbot	f	26th
Ann Talbot, Riley	f	7th	Ruth Talbot	f	26th
Francis Wragge	m	8th	Anne Chapman	f	26th
Elizabeth Thorpe	f	9th	Lydia Chapman	f	26th
Elizabeth Lowe	f	9th	Margret Allen	f	29th
Edytha Torre	f	11th	John Torre	m	29th
Anne Lowe	f	13th	Samuel Elliott	m	29th
Margaret Taylor	f	14th	Rowland Mower, Snr	m	29th
Alice Thornley	f	16th	Thomas Bocking	m	30th
Jane Naylor	f	16th	Nicholas Whiteley	m	30th
Edytha Bocking	f	17th	Jonathan Talbot	m	30th
Elizabeth Thornley	f	17th	Mary Whiteley	f	30th
Jane Talbot, Riley	f	17th	Rowland Mower	m	30th
Thomas Heald	m	18th	Joseph Allen	m	31th
George Short	m	18th	Sarah Elliott	f	31st
Catharine Talbot, Riley	f	18th	Robert Kempe	m	31st
Robert Torre	m	18th	Anne Morten	f	31st

August 1666

George Ashe	m	1st	Robert Hadfield	m	14th
Mary Naylor	f	1st	Margaret Swinnerton	f	14th
John Hadfield Snr	m	2nd	Alice Coyle	f	14th
Robert Buxton	m	2nd	Thurston Whiteley	m	15th
Anne Naylor	f	2nd	Alice Bocking	f	15th
Jonathan Naylor	m	2nd	Briget Talbot	f	15th
Elizabeth Glover	f	2nd	Michael Kempe	m	15th
Alexander Hadfield	m	3rd	Anne Wilson	f	15th
Jane Naylor	f	3rd	Thomas Bilston	m	16th
Godfrey Torre	m	3rd	Thomas Frith	m	17th
John Hancock, Jnr.	m	3rd	Joan French	f	17th
Elizabeth Hancock	f	3rd	Mary Elliott	f	17th
Margaret Buxton	f	3rd	Sarah Morten, Shepherd's Flatt	f	18th
Robert Bocking	m	3rd	Elizabeth Frith	f	18th
Thomas Hawksworth	m	4th	Anne Elliott	f	18th
Margaret Percival	f	4th	Thomas Ragge	m	18th
Anne Swinnerton	f	4th	Anne Hawksworth	f	19th

Rebecca Morten, Shepherd's Flatt	f	4th	Joan Ashmore	f	19th
Robert French	m	6th	Elizabeth Frith	f	20th
Richard Thorpe	m	6th	Margaret Morten	f	20th
Thomas Frith	m	6th	Anne Rowland	f	20th
John Elliott	m	7th	John Buxton	m	20th
Oner Hancock	f	7th	Frances Frith	f	21st
John Hancock	m	7th	Ruth Morten	f	21st
William Hancock	m	7th	— Frith (an infant)	f	22nd
Abraham Swinnerton	m	8th	Lydia Kempe	f	22nd
Alice Hancock	f	9th	Peter Hall, Bretton	m	23rd
Anne Hancock	f	10th	— Morten (an infant)	m	24th
Francis Frith	m	10th	Catherine Mompesson	f	25th
Elizabeth Kempe	f	11th	Samuel Chapman	m	25th
William Hawksworth	m	12th	Anne Frith	f	25th
Thomas Kempe	m	12th	Joan Howe	f	27th
Francis Bocking	m	13th	Thomas Ashmore	m	27th
Richard Bocking	m	13th	Thomas Wood	m	28th
Mary Bocking	f	13th	William Howe	m	30th

John Tricket	m	13th	Mary Abell	f	30th
Anne Trickett (his wife)	f	13th	Catherine Talbot	f	30th
Mary Whiteley	f	13th	Francis Wilson	m	30th
Sarah Blackwall, Bretton	f	13th			
Bridget Naylor	f	13th			

September 1666

Elizabeth Frith	f	1st	Sarah Wilson	f	10th
William Percival	m	1st	Thomas Moseley	m	13th
Robert Trickett	m	2nd	Joan Wood	f	13th
Henry Frith	m	3rd	Mary Percival	f	18th
John Wilson	m	4th	Francis Morten	m	20th
Mary Darby	f	4th	George Butterworth	m	21st
William Abell	m	7th	Anne Townsend, Bretton	f	22nd
George Frith	m	7th	Anne Glover	f	23rd
Godfrey Ashe	m	8th	Anne Hall	f	23rd
William Hawksworth	m	9th	Francis Hawksworth	m	23rd

Robert Wood, Snr	m	9th	Townsend (an infant)	f	29th
Humphrey Merrill	m	9th	Susanna Morten	f	29th

October 1666

Jonas Parsley	m	1st	Mary Morten	f	12th
Grace Morten	f	2nd	Samuel Hall	m	13th
Peter Ashe	m	4th	Peter Hall	m	13th
Abraham Morten	m	5th	Joseph Morten	m	14th
Thomas Torre Snr	m	6th	Grace Morten	f	15th
Benjamin Morten	m	6th	Elizabeth Syddall	f	17th
Elizabeth Morten	f	8th	Anne Grundy	f	17th
Alice Taylor	f	8th	Francis Morten	m	18th
Anne Parsley	f	11th	William Morten	m	28th
Agnes Sheldon	f	11th			

November 1666

Abraham Morten	m	1st

PROFILES

William Mompesson

William Mompesson was born in 1638. It is thought that his forebears were French – Mompesson being a French surname. There is some speculation that the family came over to England at the time of the Norman Conquest, and settled in Wiltshire. Robert Mompesson lived in Bathampton and married Alice – the heiress of William Godwin; they had one son, John, who became sheriff of Wiltshire. John and his wife were blessed with seven sons, Drewe, Robert, John, Thomas, Henry, William and Samuel; the family of Mompesson prospered and multiplied and were dispersed over the West of England, and it is from this line that William Mompesson was descended. The family arms are described as, 'Argent a Lion rampant sable charged on the shoulder with a martlet of the field. Crest, a jug or with a string azure, tasselled of the first. Motto: "*Ma joy en dieu seulement*".'

William's father, John Mompesson, was Vicar of Seamer near Scarborough in Yorkshire and there is a baptism recorded at Collingham, Yorkshire, on 8 (or possibly 28) April 1639. It is thought that William Mompesson was an only child, as no record can be found of any siblings.

William Mompesson attended Sherburn School in the West Riding of Yorkshire, before being accepted for and entering, at the age of sixteen, Peterhouse College, Cambridge on 16 April 1655. He was awarded a BA in 1658/59 and an MA in 1662. After gaining his MA, William followed his father's example and became a clergyman for the Church of England, accepting the post of domestic chaplain to Sir George Savile of Rufford Abbey, in Nottinghamshire.

Mompesson's first wife, Catherine Carr, was the daughter of Ralph Carr Esq., of Cocken in the County of Durham. She was a beautiful young lady, and 'possessed good parts, with exquisitely tender feelings'. Sir George Savile was informed of this marriage by his agent, William Kirk, who stated in a letter written to Sir George, dated 22 May 1661 that, 'Mr Mompesson since he came to Welley (possibly known to you) hath marryed a wife, who is now coming hither to be with him'.

Some little while later, Mompesson was appointed as Vicar of Scalby, near Scarborough, Yorkshire. In all probability, it was Sir George Savile, Lord Halifax, who was responsible for this appointment. He held this post until his patron conferred upon him the incumbency of Eyam in April 1664, following the death of the litigious rector, the Revd Shoreland Adams. Because of the parish's location, at the heart of the important lead mining industry in Derbyshire, the village was considered to be an up-and-coming rural community. When William Mompesson and his wife came to Eyam they had two young children – George and Elizabeth. It was also know that, by this time, Catherine was suffering from consumption which is now known as tuberculosis.

It appears that, initially, Mompesson did not settle down happily at Eyam; possibly because he considered that the parish was too small to give true scope for his considerable energies, or another contributory factor might have been the lack of society; but whatever the reason, or reasons, he was clearly discontented with his lot. Plague broke out in the village in September 1665, a little over a year after William Mompesson had been inducted into the living. He determined to stay in the village during the time of the pestilence, lamenting his earlier misgiving about the parish with the comment, written in a letter to his uncle:

God grant that I may repent my sad ingratitude.

At that time, Mompesson's wife implored him to leave the village until the pestilence subsided – as the squire and some of the wealthier villagers within the parish had already fled. Mompesson disregarded this plea, but tried to persuade his wife to take herself and the children to a place of safety. Equally determined, Catherine Mompesson rejected this idea, preferring to stay with her husband.

With the loss of the more prominent people within the parish, it was left to Mompesson, as rector of the parish, to co-ordinate and lead the response to the situation in which they, collectively, found themselves. Throughout the duration of the pestilence, Mompesson worked closely with a former rector of the parish, the Puritan Revd Thomas Stanley.

Mompesson and Stanley made a number of important decisions; they decided that it was better to bury the dead as soon as possible, and preferably in their own gardens or in nearby fields; that the church should be closed and Divine Worship should be conducted in the open air until the plague passed; and, their most courageous decision, they persuaded the people of the village to remain within prescribed boundaries, in order to reduce the risk of spreading the contagion to nearby villages. The self-imposed quarantine was successful, in that nobody from outside of the village died. It must however be noted that, immediately prior to the *cordon sanitaire* being agreed, William and Catherine Mompesson did, in June 1666, have their children sent away to stay with a relative in Sheffield.

Mompesson's wife died, as a direct result of the plague, on 25 August 1666. Following her death, Mompesson was distraught and feared that he too would fall victim in the near future. Previously, he had suffered from an infection to his leg but his wife had treated this successfully.

When it was believed that the pestilence had finally departed the village, William Mompesson was exhausted. In a letter to his uncle he wrote,

> *The condition of this place hath been so dreadful that I persuade myself it exceedeth all history and example. I may truely say our Town has become a Golgotha, a place of skulls; and had there not been a small remnant of us left, we had been as Sodom and like unto Gomorrah. My ears never heard such doleful lamentations. My nose never smelt such noisome smells, and my eyes never beheld such ghastly spectacles. There have been 76 families visited within my parish, out of which died 259 persons.*

In December, 1666, Mompesson's patron declared in a letter sent from London,

> *I am very glad to hear the sickness is leaving you at Eyam, which is not to be attributed to anything more than your care, excepting God Almighty's mercy to a place that hath been so long afflicted: you have been as much a Martyr all this while, as if you had died for your flock, having, besides your hazard, sacrificed the pleasure of your life to your duty for which you ought to have the reward of an eternal esteem from all good people.*

Mompesson continued his ministry in the parish of Eyam, helping to rebuild the broken community and its people. After a further three years of diligent labour, and perhaps, in part, because of the terrible price which had been paid by the families in the village he was relieved of his appointment here and transferred by Lord Savile to the markedly quieter parish of Eakring in Nottinghamshire.

During Mompesson's time at Eyam, he also held the neighbouring living of Bilsthorpe in plurality. Indeed, when he accepted the living of St Andrew's, Eakring, he continued to hold the living of Bilsthorpe.

William Mompesson remarried in 1670. His wife, Elizabeth Newby – a relative, on her mother's side, of his patron, Sir George Savile – was the widow of Charles Newby and daughter of Rowland Dand and Margaret (*née* Savile). It was in 1669, some three years after the cessation of the plague and shortly before being remarried, that William Mompesson was presented with the benefice of Eakring, near Newark, Nottinghamshire by his friend and patron, Sir George Savile. But, having come from the plague village of Eyam, he was not universally welcomed by his parishioners at Eakring, being precluded from entering both the parish church and vicarage; his parishioners being fearful that he might still be carrying the plague. There may be some vestige of truth in this legend, but there are probably more prosaic reasons as to why Mompesson was forbidden access to these buildings. From correspondence which still survives in the archives at Chatsworth House, it is known that both the church and parsonage house were in a very poor state of repair – in fact, the parsonage house was barely habitable. When examining the state of repair of the church, Mompesson found at least two breaches in the south wall of the building necessitating complete rebuilding. Also, the roof, in addition to leaking in several places, needed a number of new supports because of decaying timbers. He also found that several window frames and the glazing therein needed immediate remedial attention, as did the floor paving in the church. He blamed this poor state of repair on the previous incumbent, the Revd George Lawson, and subsequently sued his widow for the dilapidations in the Church Court at York. Having won his case but still having insufficient funds to complete the repairs, Mompesson appealed to the Savile and Pierrepont Lords of the two Eakring Manors. The resulting shortfall, which amounted to somewhat in excess of £60, was met by Mompesson himself. It is believed that he personally contributed considerably more than this sum in order to render the parsonage house habitable.

During the time that the church and parsonage house were being refurbished, Mompesson and his wife were obliged to live in a house which she owned in nearby Rufford Park, which was on the Savile Estate. The newly married couple stayed there, where it is believed they lived in relative seclusion, until the repairs to the parsonage house had been effected and the fear of infection from the plague had also died away. William Mompesson and his new wife were not able to enter the parsonage house until early in 1671.

Incorporated into the plans for the rebuilding of the church, Mompesson had the nave widened, porches built to the north and south and, prior to completion in 1674, a pulpit and font were added. Also at this time, the coat of arms of Charles II adorned the church. It graced the church for upwards of 200 years, until falling victim to dampness. For the considerable time that the church was being restored, Mompesson was forced to hold divine services in a field almost a mile distant from the village itself. His sermons were preached from under an ash tree rising from a small hillock. The tree subsequently became known as Pulpit Ash.

William and Elizabeth Mompesson had four children: two daughters – Eliza and Jane – and two sons, both of whom died in infancy.

In 1676 Mompesson became a Prebendary Canon of Southwell; where it is said he was an active member of the Chapter. He was also active in the rebuilding of the prebendial houses there; an action which was necessitated by damage caused during the time of the Rebellion. Some time later he became a Prebend of York. Thankful people wished to confer further honours upon him, including that of the Deanery of Lincoln, but Mompesson refused these as he now desired a somewhat quieter life. He was, however, instrumental in ensuring that his friend and colleague, Dr Fuller, was offered the appointment.

William Mompesson died on 7 March 1708, after having been rector of Eakring for thirty-eight years. He died in the seventieth year of his age. He is buried in Eakring Church where a brass plate in the church bears a Latin inscription, which

> marks the place in the chancel, at Eakring, where his ashes repose. Though his tomb may moulder in the dust, and be forgotten, yet his memorial of humanity and devotedness to his afflicted parishioners will never perish.

Also, there are three stained-glass windows in the church, which bear the inscription

> To the Glory of God and to perpetuate the memory of William Mompesson, priest, rector of this parish for 38 years, and previously Rector of Eyam in Derbyshire, where he faithfully ministered to his flock during the terrible Plague which raged, 1665–6, the three small windows in this chancel are dedicated.

In 1893, the then Lord Savile of Rufford Abbey commissioned a memorial stone cross to be erected on the site of the Pulpit Ash, to serve as a timely reminder of the unusual circumstances which marked Mompesson's arrival in Eakring – the original ash tree having fallen during a strong gale. Eakring Parish Council had the cross cleaned in 1965 and also built a pathway to ease access to the memorial. An ash sapling has also been planted at the location of the original ash tree.

Thomas Stanley

Thomas Stanley was born in the small village of Duckmanton, some three miles from Chesterfield. He was educated at Netherthorpe Grammar School, Staveley, before entering St John's College, Cambridge, where he took the degree of MA in his twenty-second year. Stanley began as a Churchman upon graduating, being employed by a family in a tutorial capacity, before beginning his ecclesiastical ministry as curate to the elder Cart, rector of Handsworth. He then spent a further three years as preacher and curate at Dore Chapel which, at that time, was in the parish of Dronfield. A further eight years were then spent at Ashford-in-the-Water.

In 1644, during the time of the Civil War, the Revd Thomas Stanley was translated to the living of Eyam, following the arrest of the bona-fide rector, Shoreland Adams, who held Royalist views which could not be countenanced by the ruling Puritans. However, at the Restoration of the Monarchy in 1660, when King Charles II was returned to the throne, Stanley was removed and the previous incumbent, the Revd Shoreland Adams, was reinstated. Immediately upon the return of Adams, it is thought that Stanley stayed in the parish and fulfilled his role within the community as he had done previously, albeit in an auxiliary capacity, giving help, support and spiritual sustenance to his former parishioners. It is also believed that, on the frequent occasions when the Revd Shoreland Adams was residing in his preferred parish of Treeton in Yorkshire, Stanley acted as curate within the parish; a duty which he performed until the Act of Uniformity was passed in 1662. This Act required that 'every parson, vicar or other minister whatsoever' should, before the Feast of St Bartholomew, 'openly and publicly before the congregation assembled for religious worship, declare his unfeigned assent and consent to all and everything contained in, and prescribed by, the Book of Common Prayer.' Also enshrined in the Act was the statement that 'no person should be capable of any benefice, or presume to consecrate or administer the Holy Sacrament, before he ordained a Priest by Episcopal ordination'. The requirements of the Act ensured that any minister who did not adhere to these terms would be deprived of their livings and if they officiated in any church, they would be subject to fines and imprisonment. It was, primarily, because of this and other associated Acts that Stanley, together with 2,000 other clergy left their pulpits and resigned their livings on St Bartholomew's Day, 24 August, 1662; profoundly disagreeing with the Acts and the introduction of the new Book of Common Prayer. However, having been dispossessed of his living, because of his doctrinal differences with the Established Church, his sympathies with Parliament and the demands imposed upon him by the terms of the so-called Five Mile Act, the Corporation Act and

the Act of Uniformity, Stanley continued to preach in private houses in
Eyam, Hazleford and some other places.

The ramifications of the Acts were particularly punitive, their
enforcement coming, effectively, immediately prior to the time when
the yearly tithes were payable to the incumbent. The net effect of this
measure was to ensure that clergy were dispossessed of their livings, and
immediately forced to seek alternative sources of income. At that time
Stanley, a staunch Puritan, departed the village.

Following his ejection from the Established Church and the loss of his
living at Eyam, an undated 'humble petition and certificate', thought to be
sent sometime in 1661/62, witnessed or signed by sixty-nine freeholders
and other villagers of Eyam, was sent to Sir George Savile. The petition
stated,

> *Humbly shewing and declaringe that one Shorland Adams about twenty
> years since was minister at Eyam aforesaid and that duringe the tyme
> hee continued as minister there your petitioners well knows and humbly
> certifie that the said Mr Adams was scandalous in life, negligent and
> idle in preachinge, of a turbulent and Contentious spirit and proud
> behaviour, to our great prejudice and discouragement; with all of which
> your honourable father was well acquainted and declared himselfe much
> displeased with the Carriage and Course of life of the said Mr Adams, for
> which Cause and for that the said Mr Adams then held and enjoyed the
> parsonage of Treeton in the County of Yorke, the said Mr Adams shortly
> afterwards left Eyam, and being then destitute of a minister, through
> the mercy of God, and assistance of our friends, we procured one Mr
> Thomas Stanley an able, peaceable pyous orthodox Devine to be our
> minister, who hath Continued with us ever since and Diligently Carefully
> and Constantly hath preached and taught amongst us, by whose pyous
> preachinge and painefull instruction wee have received much comfort to
> our Soules, and by the good Example of his holy and peaceable life are
> much encouraged.*
>
> *Wherefore wee humbly beseech your honour (beinge informed that it
> is in your power only) to Continue and settle the said Mr Stanley to be
> our minister at Eyam aforesaid and thereby you will bring much glory
> to God and Comfort to our Soules, and for which wee shall ever prayse
> God and pray for your honour's happiness.*

At this period there was much unrest about religious beliefs and the manner
in which churches conducted their affairs. And, more locally within the
parish of Eyam, there were divergent opinions as regards the ministry
of the Revd Thomas Stanley. It cannot be denied that there were many

people within the village with whom Stanley was unpopular because of the Nonconformist beliefs which he espoused. Indeed, this faction within the parish actively agitated for his ejection from Eyam.

Following the death of the Revd Shoreland Adams 11 April 1664, a new rector was appointed – the Revd William Mompesson. Also at this time, Stanley's devoted wife, Anne, died; she was buried at Eyam on 14 June 1664. Her death came as a bitter blow and caused him much grieving. Having now returned to the village, Stanley, the Nonconformist, became friendly with Mompesson, the Conformist, and, although holding diametrically opposing views regarding church teaching and liturgy, they were, however, able to work together, accepting that it was infinitely better to work for the common good in these unprecedented times. Indeed, as the pestilence took hold in the parish during the following year, Stanley and Mompesson worked very closely together, so closely in fact that, through their combined endeavours seeking to unite the several different religious factions within the parish, they were able to gain agreement on a number of far-reaching sanctions which they sought to implement in the village in order to mitigate the fear of spreading the contagious disease; they decided that it was better to bury the dead as soon as possible, and preferably in their own gardens or in nearby fields; that the church should be closed and Divine Worship should be conducted in the open air until the plague passed; and, their bravest decision, they persuaded the people of the village to remain within prescribed boundaries, in order to reduce the risk of spreading the contagion to nearby villages. It is improbable that, considering the different religious factions within the village, the actions being suggested would have been accepted and implemented without parishioners witnessing that both religious leaders were of the same belief in advocating the measures. The self-imposed quarantine and *cordon sanitaire* was successful as that nobody from outside of the village died. It is undoubtedly the case that, because of the joint labours of these two ministers, a degree of acceptance was re-established in the village, enabling these important decisions to be taken and acted upon. During the time of the plague, Mompesson and Stanley worked ceaselessly in the parish, both day and night, caring for the sick and dying, and enjoying little respite or relaxation. However, many people are of the view that it was Stanley who exerted himself during the plague more than Mompesson, and that it was mainly due to Stanley's ministrations that the inhabitants of Eyam did not suffer to greater extent and that it was him who was mainly instrumental in ensuring that the contagion did not spread to neighbouring towns and villages. There appear to be grounds suggesting that Stanley has not received the justice which he should be accorded. And now, with the benefit of almost 400 years of hindsight, it seems odious that one of these brave men continues to be viewed with total approbation and esteem, whereas the other, who performed equally heroic endeavours, continues to be ostracised.

In 1702, the Revd William Bagshaw, who was an assistant minister in Sheffield and curate at Attercliffe, published his *De Spiritualibus Pecci* and in an extract, which he quoted from Calamy's *Lives of the Nonconformists*, it is abundantly clear as to the esteem in which Stanley was held by the parishioners of Eyam. The extract reads:

> *He was an eminent Preacher; and a very vifible and audible Confuter, of thofe who adventure to decry free conceived Prayer; faying, there is no fuch Gift, whereby Perfons can fuit their Prayers to Divine Povidence, and their own and others particular Cafes. When he could not ferve his People Publickly, he was helpful to them in Private; efpecially, when the Peftilence prevail'd in that Town. He Officiated amongft them with great Tendernefs and Affection, during that Sore and very Mortal Vifitation, which in that little Place cut off 259 grown Perfons, and 58 Children. And yet even at that very Time did fome who might have been better employ'd, make a Motion to the Lord-Lieutenant of the County, the Noble Earl, Grandfather of the prefent Illuftrious Duke of Devonfhire, to remove him out of Town. Who like himfelf, made fuch Reply as this; That it was more reafonable, that Thankfulnefs to him, who together with his Care of the Town had taken fuch Care, as none elfe did, to prevent the Infection of the Towns adjacent.*

It is a matter of record that Thomas Stanley had at least one son, John. He was educated at Tideswell Grammar School, which had been founded by Bishop Pursglove in 1579. John Stanley later studied at St John's College, Cambridge – the same college from where his father had graduated. Following his graduation, John Stanley was appointed as a member of staff at Tideswell Grammar School. In 1678 he deputised for the Headmaster, John Rowarth, who had been given 'a special license to absent himself in order that he might take a degree at the University of Cambridge'.

Stanley's health began to fail, and he died on St Bartholomew's Day 1670, the eighth anniversary of his deposition from his living at Eyam. He was buried in the village on 26 August, although the exact burial place is unknown.

> *He dy'd in 1670, fatisfy'd to the laft in the Caufe of Nonconformity, and rejoicing in his Sufferings on that Account.*

When considering the circumstances surrounding his friend's death, the Revd William Bagshaw – the 'Apostle of the Peak' – wrote,

Poor I was on a Sabbath night called out of my bed (as I remember) to visit him whom I found in a desirable frame of spirit, tho' weak in body, as I also found that, tho' on account of his Nonconformity he had suffered much, he rejoiced that he suffered in (and for) that cause. Within three days, even on St. Bartholomew's Day (still called black), he expired.

The Revd William Bagshaw was not permitted to conduct the service of interment, but received permission to preach a funeral sermon to the memory of his friend and colleague; his texts were taken from Zechariah chapter one, verse five, 'Your fathers, where [are] they? and the prophets, do they live for ever?', and Isaiah 57:1, 'The righteous perisheth, and no man layeth [it] to heart: and merciful men [are] taken away, none considering that the righteous is taken away from the evil [to come]'. Also during his sermon, the Revd Bagshaw paid the following tribute to Stanley:

His diligence in studying, and his zeal in sound, plain, practical preaching were worthy of (what they met with) a remark ... He was a great encourager of week-day lectures, by his preaching at 'em and by his presence when his Juniors or Seniors preached ... He was a very visible and audible confutor of those who venture to deny free conceived prayer, adventuring to say there is no such gift ...

In 1868/69, the north aisle of the church at Eyam was rebuilt to mark the bicentenary of the passing of the plague and also the heroism of the rector, Revd William Mompesson, and a former incumbent of the parish, the Revd Thomas Stanley. The brass plaque affixed to the wall bears the inscription:

This Memorial Aisle was erected by Voluntary Contributions obtained in 1866, to commemorate the Christian and Heroic virtues of the Revd W. Mompesson (rector), Catharine his Wife, and the Revd T. Stanley (late rector). When this place was visited by the Plague in 1665–6, they steadfastly continued to succour the afflicted and to minister amongst them the Truths and consolations of the Gospel of Jesus Christ. The rebuilding and enlarging of the Aisle led to the restoration of almost the entire Church, in 1868–9, at the cost of £2160.

There is now a memorial stone in the churchyard at Eyam dedicated to the memory of the Revd Thomas Stanley, even though he is not buried there.

Catherine Mompesson, *née* Carr

Catherine Mompesson, *née* Carr was the daughter of Ralph Carr Esq., of Cocken, in the County of Durham. She was baptised on 17 Dec 1633 at Medomsley, Durham. She married William Mompesson, but the exact date of the wedding is not known. She was a beautiful young lady, and 'possessed good parts, with exquisitely tender feelings'. However, in a letter written from Rufford on 22 May 1661, Sir George Savile was notified of the wedding by his agent, William Kirk. In the letter, Kirk stated that 'Mr Mompesson since he came to Welley (possibly known to you) hath marryed a wife, who is now coming hither to be with him'.

Catherine Mompesson came to Eyam in April 1664, when her husband was inducted into the parish. But, before coming to Eyam, Mompesson held an appointment at Scalby, near Scarborough, where the list of incumbents includes 'Wm. Mompesson, clerk, afterwards Rector of Eyam, Derbys,' and is dated 1662–63. At the time of their arrival at Eyam, Catherine and William Mompesson had two children, George and Elizabeth. Also by that time, it had been confirmed that Catherine was ill. It is thought that she was suffering from consumption – now known as tuberculosis.

At the outbreak of the plague, Catherine tried to persuade her husband that the family should vacate the parish for the duration of the pestilence – as many other leading families in the village had done. William did not accede to this request, but agreed that their children should be sent to relatives in Yorkshire. He also suggested that she should join them, but Catherine would not leave William's side at this difficult time. She was devoted to William and worked with him, tirelessly, distributing medication, plague remedies and giving strength and support to needy parishioners.

On one of their regular evening walks in the fields by the rectory, Catherine declared 'Oh, Mompesson, the air! How sweet it smells!' Unfortunately, Mompesson knew exactly what that comment signalled. The next morning it was confirmed that Catherine Mompesson was in the throes of the plague. Catherine died at the height of the epidemic and was buried in the churchyard on 25 August 1666.

During the 'Plague Sunday' commemoration service which has been held every year since 1905, a bouquet of red roses is placed on her tomb.

Marshall Howe

Marshall Howe was a local lead miner who lived in the village of Eyam at the time of the plague. When the distemper visited the parish, because of its unprecedented virulence, and also the fear of the contagion spreading, people were reluctant and disinclined to bury their dead. It was at this time that Marshall Howe took it upon himself to act as self-appointed sextant. He was not fearful of catching the disease himself, as he had suffered and survived the plague some while ago and thus considered himself to be immune from further attacks. When people were exhorted to bury their own dead – and, furthermore, to bury them in their own land rather than the churchyard, which had now been closed – Howe willingly offered his services. He was a physically large and strong man, some described him as being gigantic, and because of his immunity he was not afraid of performing the task which others couldn't face. It soon became voiced abroad that Marshall Howe was ready and able to bury the dead, even though, throughout the whole period, his wife pleaded with him to cease his perilous avocation. However, the rewards were too great for Howe to resist. His preferred method of disposal was to make an initial assessment of the spoils he might gain from his labours; and then, having made his assessment, he would dig a shallow grave before tying a length of rope around the foot or neck of the corpse – whichever was easier – and in that way, he didn't have to touch it when dragging it to the newly dug grave. Having finished his labours for the day, he would collect his rewards and then repair to the local hostelry, where he would boast to the assembled persons by declaring that 'He had pinners and napkins sufficient to kindle his pipe with while he lived'.

Howe's labours continued, unabated, for in excess of two months and, during that time, he disposed of several putrid and rotting plague-ridden bodies. Also, it was reported that there were some occasions when Howe was seen to be burying people who had barely drawn their last breath; indeed, the story is told of one occasion when Howe was called to the home of a recently deceased person, a certain Edward Unwin. Following his usual practice, Howe first dug a shallow grave on Unwin's land, and then proceeded up the stairs to bring the, still warm, corpse down. Halfway down the stairs, a loud cry emanated from the corpse, followed by the words, 'I want a posset'. It was at this point that Howe realised that the 'corpse' was still alive! He immediately dropped the body from where it had been draped around his shoulders and swiftly departed the homestead. Receiving his posset some little while later, Edward Unwin recovered and went on to live to a ripe old age.

This event did not however deter Howe from his chosen calling, that is, until his own wife Joan was taken with the distemper. It was only at that time, when Howe saw the telltale buboes appear on her bosom, that he became painfully aware that it might have been himself who had brought the pestilence across his own threshold. After a short but painful illness,

Joan Howe died on the morning of Monday 27 August 1666. Howe buried her with a degree of dignity and circumspection that he had not previously demonstrated at other burials. But, more tragedy was to befall the now hapless Howe. On his return home, he found that his only son, William, was now exhibiting the first manifestations of the plague. William, who had inherited much of his father's strong constitution, fought the deadly disease for three long fever-ridden days. The inevitable end came on Thursday 30 August 1666 and he was buried by his grieving father alongside the grave of his mother. Following the deaths of his wife and son, Howe buried many more people in the parish before the distemper finally departed; but with a little more care than he had previously shown.

Marshall Howe continued to live in the parish for many years after the plague had departed, and was laid to rest on 20 April 1698. But, for some generations after the plague, parents in Eyam would still threaten to send for Marshall Howe if their children misbehaved.

SOME PLACES OF INTEREST
NEAR TO EYAM

Bakewell

The small market town of Bakewell in the Derbyshire Dales, and the only town in the Peak District National Park, has a history dating back to Anglo-Saxon times, although there is evidence to suggest that there was a prehistoric Iron Age settlement in this area somewhat before that time. The town, which was in the Anglian kingdom of Mercia, grew around a number of wells and warm springs and was called Badecan Wiellon, a name meaning 'Badeca's Well'. The Anglo-Saxon Chronicle of 924 states that Edward the Elder built a 'burgh' along the valley of the River Wye and later, in Norman times, a motte-and-bailey castle were built above the main river crossing. The original fords across the river were replaced by bridges, the 800-year-old five-arch bridge and the Holme packhorse bridge which has been used since 1664. Traders coming from the direction of Monyash used the bridge in order to avoid paying the taxes imposed if entering in the centre of the town. The bridge was of such dimensions that it was possible for a packhorse, carrying upwards of two hundredweight of produce, to cross the river. The manor of Badequella and its parish church are both mentioned in the Domesday Book of 1086, which stated that there was land for eight ploughs, thirty-three villagers and nine smallholders.

The town of Bakewell lies on the banks of the River Wye, being some thirty miles to the north of the county town of Derby, seven miles to the south of Eyam and thirteen miles to the south-west of Sheffield. Bakewell's immediate neighbouring towns being Chesterfield, which lies to the east, and Buxton which lies, roughly, in a north-westerly direction.

The parish church of All Saints, Bakewell, is a Grade I listed building. A church was founded on this site in 920, and an intricately carved

Anglo-Saxon cross can still be seen in the churchyard. The present church was built in the twelfth and thirteenth centuries. It is possible that there were Christian settlers in the area during the Roman occupation; however, it is a matter of record that there was a church in Bakewell as early as Anglo-Saxon times. The Christian faith, having faded, was rekindled by Celtic missionaries coming from Northumbria towards the end of the seventh century. A number of 'minsters' were built in the area and Bakewell was one of these.

Danish invaders wreaked further destruction, so a new church was built in the tenth century on the site of the old church. By this time, the town of Bakewell was assuming some prominence in the area, so much so that it is recorded in the Domesday Book that the church was able to support two priests, one of only two such churches in Derbyshire.

The manor of Bakewell was granted to William Peverel by William the Conqueror; it is thought that William Peverel was one of William the Conqueror's many illegitimate children. A new church was built in Bakewell by Peverel – evidence of which can still be seen today. But, significant changes were made to the church's structure in the mid-thirteenth century. This restructuring remodelled the church to the Early English style, with a widened north aisle, and the heavier rounded Norman arches were replaced with lancet arches which were of a lighter design. There was also substantial rebuilding to the south transept, which became 'new work' or 'Newark'. Later, the chancel at the east end of the church was extended. The following century saw further significant changes; a tower, spire and south porch were added, as were buttresses and battlements. But, with the passage of time, it became self-evident during the eighteenth century that the spire and tower were too heavy to be supported, as there was buckling and cracking developing in the structure. The church spire was removed in 1825, and an urgent appraisal was made of the state of repair of the church in general. As a result, plans were drawn for a new church to be built on the site but, in the event, the decision was taken to rebuild the existing church. In 1839, under the direction of the Sheffield architect William Flockton, the crossing and transept were rebuilt and strengthened so that a new tower and spire could be built. Also, the medieval font was relocated to a new baptistery in the south-west of the church. Later on, the chancel was remodelled; a new mosaic floor was laid and a new reredos and high altar installed.

Much of the stained glass in the church dates from the late nineteenth century. Henry Holiday's 'Lamb of God' window in the north aisle is one of the church's treasures.

There are two stone crosses in the grounds of the parish church. One cross, known as the Bakewell Cross and thought to have been carved in the seventh or eighth century, stands some eight feet high. A number of scenes are depicted on the cross including the Annunciation. Originally, the cross is thought to have stood at the Hassop Cross Roads. The other cross, possibly dating from the tenth or eleventh century and known as the Beeley Cross or Two Dales Cross, is considered by many to have been dug up in a field near to Beeley. It is believed that the cross was then moved to the grounds of Holt House near Darley Bridge. The cross itself, of which only the lower half of the shaft survives, stands about five feet high and is carved on all four faces.

It was in the small village of Ashford-in-the-Water, less than two miles from Bakewell, that the Revd Thomas Stanley spent eight years as curate before being translated to the living of Eyam in 1644.

A market was established in the town as early as 1254 and, resulting from this, Bakewell developed into a centre for trading. In order to accommodate the increased trade which was now coming to the town, a five-arch bridge was built across the River Wye. In 1330, King Edward III granted a market charter to the town. The traditional market was and, 700 years later, still is held on Monday; it's a day when livestock, general provisions and other domestic comestibles are traded. In 1998 the Agricultural Business Centre was opened and much of the market activity switched from the Market Square, although there is still a stall market held in the town centre.

Located towards the far end of Bath Gardens, and across from Rutland Square is the Bakewell Bath House. A spring containing iron salts, a so-called chalybeate spring, was found in the area, and as a result the Bath House was built in 1697. As the Duke of Rutland was intent on establishing Bakewell as a spa town emulating Buxton and Matlock, he ensured that the building was fitted with every convenience, including a shower, pool and a reading room. However, the water from the spring had a temperature of 15°C, which was considerably colder than that of its neighbouring competitors, and, as a result, the venture ultimately ended in failure.

In 1777, Richard Arkwright leased land, near to the River Wye, from Philip Gell, where he later built a cotton-spinning factory at Lumford Mill in 1782. The mill was managed by Arkwright's son, Richard Arkwright junior, and was a prosperous concern, employing at its peak somewhere in the region of 350 persons, most of whom were women and children. The mill was sold to the Duke of Devonshire but eight years later it was burnt down. The mill was rebuilt and continued in operation until the end of the century. The site of the original mill is now known as Riverside Business Park Ltd and is still one of the largest industrial estates in the National Park, housing upwards of forty local businesses.

The building of Lumford Mill, coupled with improvements in infrastructure, prompted further development within the town, and a number of cotton mills were built, although the traditional industries of lead mining and farming were still central to the town's economy.

With ever-increasing prosperity, Bakewell railway station was opened in 1862 by the Manchester, Buxton, Matlock & Midlands Junction Railway. The line subsequently became part of the Midland Railway and later still, a section of the main line from London to Manchester built by the London, Midland & Scottish Railway Company (LMS). John Ruskin is reputed to have had strong objections to what he considered to be the desecration of the Derbyshire countryside, declaring that 'a Buxton fool may be able to find himself in Bakewell in twelve minutes, and vice versa'.

The proposed route to be taken by the railway line necessitated it passing through the Duke of Rutland's estate at Haddon Hall. The duke acquiesced to the proposed route and – because an Act of Parliament was necessary to allow the building of railway lines – agreed to support its passage through parliament, on the understanding that the line itself would be out of sight of Haddon Hall, that the station buildings would be located on the hillside some way out of the town and that carved into the building's stonework would be the duke's personal coat of arms. The disused line has now been transformed into the Monsal Trail; a track specifically dedicated for walking, cycling and horse riding.

Today, Bakewell is a thriving town and tourist centre. As the largest town in the Peak District, the town boasts many tourist attractions within easy reach, including; Haddon Hall, Chatsworth House and Farm Shop, Gulliver's Kingdom and Heights of Abraham at Matlock Bath, Wirksworth Heritage Centre, Peak Rail steam trains, Peveril Castle and Crich Tramway Village. There are also many small independent stores and boutiques, including camping and outdoor shops, and outlets for antiques, stamps, books, fishing, music and interior design. Many outdoor activities can also be enjoyed, including; walking, biking, climbing, golf and riding. There are also abundant restaurants, bistros, cafés and public houses in the town. Traditional well dressing takes place during June. There are colourful displays, made from flower petals, seeds and tree bark embedded into panels of wet clay, and placed at various locations in the town. The Bakewell Agricultural Show, dating back to 1819, and often referred to as the 'Little Royal', is one of the largest covered agricultural shows in Britain. The two-day show is held during the first week in August at the Bakewell Showground. The Bakewell Arts Festival, which started in 1997, is also held in August. In May, Bakewell hosts the Spring Peak Literary Festival and there is an autumn festival held in October. Bakewell also has a carnival week in July, which culminates in a procession though the town.

Bakewell is also the home of the eponymous pudding. However, there is much conjecture and divergence of opinion as to where the original 'secret' recipe of the famous Bakewell Pudding resides – but, by popular consent, it is now generally agreed that the original pudding was made by accident in 1820. A certain Mrs Greaves, who was at that time the landlady of a coaching inn, the White Horse Inn – now known as the Rutland Arms – was expecting some special guests at dinner. However, during the preparation of the dinner, she was called away on other business, so left instructions with her cook to make a pudding with an egg mixture, an almond paste pastry base and strawberry jam on the top. But the cook was inexperienced and misunderstood Mrs Greaves instructions; instead of mixing the eggs and almond paste into the pastry she spread it on the top of the jam. During cooking the jam rose through the paste, and the pudding thus became a tart and not a pudding! When served, all of the guests praised the dish, so Mrs Greaves instructed her staff to continue preparing the dish in the same way – it was destined to become a huge success at the inn, and the tradition continues to this day! There are two shops in Bakewell claiming to offer the original recipe, 'Bloomers Old and Only Original' and 'The Old Original Bakewell Pudding Shop'.

The Old House Museum in Cunningham Place (Tel: 01629 813642), just behind All Saints church, was originally a parsonage, but now houses a wheelwright's shop, a mill worker's dwelling, a draper's, a Victorian kitchen and a blacksmith's shop. The M&C Motorcycle Museum in Matlock Street, DE45 1EE (Tel: 01629 815011) is another of the town's many interesting museums.

Bakewell Old Town Hall, built in 1709 and situated in King Street, is always a popular visitor attraction. For many years, in addition to being the town hall and butter market, the upper floor was used as a Court and Quarter Sessions, and then from 1826 until 1874 the upper floor became the premises of Lady Manners' Grammar School. After that, from 1885 until 1964, it became a Working Men's Club. Up until 1964 the ground floor was used as a fish and game shop, but the building has also housed during its chequered history an antiques showroom and a fire station!

Behind the Old Town Hall are the Bakewell Almshouses which are also well worth seeing. The almshouses were founded by deeds, dated 30 April 1602 and 26 April 1605 by Roger Manners and John Manners of Haddon Hall; 'so that we can give charitable disposition towards the relief of poor people inhabiting the town of Bakewell.' Income to support the dwelling was to be raised from rents levied on lands at Bradmore in South Nottinghamshire. The 1602 provision made accommodation available for four men, with each receiving a small pension. It was described as 'so much of a newly erected house, being part of the chapel, as contained four lodgings below and having the Town Hall over it, and the backside or garden-stead and shall remain a hospital for ever and the same should be called St John's Hospital'. The provision was increased to accommodate six men in 1605. Also at that time their pension was increased, as was the allowance given to the laundress who lived elsewhere!

Certain stipulations were made, which had to be adhered to by the Almsmen. For instance, Almsmen were to be 'single and unmarried and wear a gown, upon the left breast of which was a cross of blue and yellow to be continually worn'. Also, in the event of an inmate being 'an alehouse haunter, drunkard or notorious offender or found begging' he was to be expelled. And the conditions of tenure didn't end there; it was mandatory for all Almsmen to attend church, failure to do so would result in a fine of 12 pence.

The Tourist Information Centre is located in Old Market Hall, Bridge Street DE45 1DS (Tel/Fax: 01629 813227. Email: bakewell@peakdistrict-npa.gov.uk). However, before the Old Market Hall was converted to a tourist information and visitor centre, it had a series of different uses including being a dance hall, library and, at one time, a wash house.

There is ample car parking space around the Agricultural Business Centre, Coombs Road, Market Street, Granby Road and Bakewell Station.

Hope

The ancient settlement of Hope lies about a mile and a half due east of its neighbour Castleton and in the centre of the broad alluvial Hope Valley to the north of the county – at the confluence of the River Noe and Peakshole Water, within the Peak National Park. The village lends its name to the Hope Valley, which stretches for about six miles with Castleton at the western end and Hathersage at the other. Looking to the north there is Lose Hill and Win Hill, and the heather-covered moors of the Dark Peak. Looking in a southerly direction are the limestone dales of the so-called White Peak. The main thoroughfare lies along the Castleton to Sheffield road, but there is also much development along Edale Road, which runs at right angles. The valley lies in an east–west orientation at the boundary between the gritstone moors of the Dark Peak, which contrasts with the deep cut dales and limestone outcrops of the White Peak. The village is referred to in the Domesday survey of 1086.

Hope, which means 'a valley', is steeped in history – there being evidence of dwellings in this area since the Ancient Britons. After their time, the area was populated by the Celts and then the Romans, and later still came the Anglo-Saxons and then the Danes. Tradition maintains that Lose Hill and Win Hill, gained their names from a battle which took place in AD 626. Battle lines were drawn, with King Cuicholm of Wessex encamped on one hill and King Edwin of Northumbria on the other. It appears that the army from Wessex far outnumbered the men from Northumbria. Edwin, realising these differences and being an astute commander, ordered his troops to build a wall of stone around the summit of the hill before battle commenced. Then, at the start of battle, both sides advanced but, having superior numbers, the Wessex troops started to push back King Edwin's troops. Sensing victory, the Wessex army were given the command to charge, only to be met by a barrage of boulders being hurled down from the top of the hill – hence, Win Hill and Lose Hill!

To the east of the village, in the hamlet of Brough-on-Noe, there is evidence of a wooden fort which was built by the Roman Governor Agricola in AD 78. The fort, known as Anavio or Navio, was a little west of the village of Brough-on-Noe near to Hope – brough being an old English word meaning fort. As the Romans were under frequent attack from the native Brigante tribe, they rebuilt the fort in stone some eighty years later. The fort was of strategic significance, protecting, as it did, Roman lead-mining interests in the Peak District. In more recent times, a section of Roman road has been uncovered just south of the Parish Church. The road probably connected the fort to the Portway. There is a nearby field known as 'Burgate', which means, 'road to the fort'.

There were castles at both Hope and Castleton, with Hope pre-dating Peveril Castle at Castleton by 100 years. However, little remains of Hope Castle apart from an earthen mound which can be seen from Pindale Road.

Turnpike roads to Sheffield and Chapel-en-le-Frith were built in the early part of the nineteenth century. Then, in 1820, the Glossop Road which went through Ashopton and the Woodlands was opened. Previous to this, and right up until the time of the Battle of Waterloo, packhorses travelled along the various bridle paths leading from Chesterfield and Sheffield through the Peaks to Stockport and Manchester. Winnats Pass, a collapsed limestone cavern, is the only road giving access from the west, now that road down from Mam Tor has been swept away.

The village of Hope stands at the crossroads of the Chapel-en-le-Frith to Sheffield road, the A625, and the Tideswell to Edale road, the B6049. This latter road follows the Portway, the old trading route which ran the length of the county from north to south. It is possible that the village originated at the crossing of the Portway and the prehistoric east-west route. In later medieval times this route was used by Jaggers – a local term for men driving packhorses carrying salt, cheese and other commodities from Cheshire. Saltergate Lane, Salter Barn, Salto Lane and Jaggers Lane can still found in the area.

In December 1272, permission was given by Edward I to build Hope Hall. The building, being relatively small, was later knocked down and a new hall erected on the same site. The hall was completed in 1508 and then extended in 1729. The Balguy family, who were landowners in the area, lived there for many generations. In 1715 the squire, John Balguy, obtained a charter to hold a weekly cattle market within the grounds of the hall. The market is now held on alternate Wednesdays and there is also a fair which is held on or near to the old May Day, 13 May. In former times, this was the day of the Statutes Fair, when farm labourers and other working men lined up and offered themselves for hire for the coming year. The practice was discontinued in the mid-nineteenth century when the Revd Wilmot C. B. Cave was Vicar of Hope. The Market Place stands opposite the church.

Many families of Derbyshire trace their roots to Hope, including the Eyres. In the reign of Henry III, William Le Eyr of Hope held lands there, as did his son Robert Le Eyr of Hope during the reign of Edward I – both holding the title Foresters of Fee, under the chief official or bailiff. In the fifteenth century, Robert, the third son of Nicholas Eyre of Hope, married the heiress Joan de Padley.

Not far from the village is the site of one of the valley's major employers, Hope cement works. At first sight it may appear incongruous that a manufacturing facility of this type is located in such a picturesque area, but the decision to build the works was dictated by geology. To the south and west there are large deposits of limestone, which can be quarried with relative ease, and to the north and east there are large amounts shale – both materials being necessary elements in the manufacturing process; and so in 1929, and without the necessity of major infrastructure upheaval, the facility was opened by G. & T. Earle. This development came many years before the concept of a National Park had been floated. In the 1960s, because of the need to increase output from the plant, the facility was expanded under the then owners the Blue Circle group of companies. In 2001 the Lafarge Group acquired Blue Circle Industries plc.

The train from Liverpool to Sheffield, and beyond to the east coast has become a popular method of seeing and visiting the valley; a very different picture from when the Midland Railway first arrived in the Hope Valley in 1894. Today, trains emerging from the Cowburn tunnel stop at Edale, Hope, Bamford and Hathersage. In former times, not only did they bring visitors from many of the surrounding towns and cities, they also brought an influx of construction workers who were employed to build the Howden and Derwent Dams. The workers lived at Birchinlee, a 'Tin

Town' built especially for them. After the dams were completed many of the workers stayed on and made Hope their home. There was further housing development along Castleton Road in the 1920s, when the Hope Cement Works was being built.

Hope is the only church in North Derbyshire mentioned in the Domesday survey of 1086, when upwards of two thirds of the Royal Forest of the High Peak fell within the parish bounds as did the seven berewicks of Edale, Aston, Shatton, half of Offerton, Tideswell, Stoke and Muchedswelle. The manor formed part of the extensive domains granted by the Conqueror to William Peveril in 1068. Hope is also one of the oldest centres of Christianity in the region, having borne witness to that faith for over 1,000 years. The parish was unusual, in that it was recorded as having both a church and a priest. It is known that there was a church here before the Norman Conquest and occupying the same site that St Peter's parish church stands on today. Sadly, as a result of rebuilding in the fourteenth century, only the Norman font remains. It was during this period of rebuilding that the church gained its distinctive stubby broach-spire.

In 1643 Parliament ordered that 'all crosses in any open place were to be removed and destroyed'. It appears that the enforcement of this order during the Puritan regime, may account for an ancient cross being used as building material in the reconstruction of the schoolhouse in 1655.

Until very recent times, the ancient parish of Hope was one of the largest in England and also one of the most important in Derbyshire with registers dating back to February 1598. The parish included Fairfield, which is now a part of Buxton; the district around the Snake Inn known as the Woodlands or Hope Woodlands; Shall-cross and Fernilee in the valley of the Goyt beyond Chapel-en-le-Frith; the present parish of Bradwell; and, in ancient times, Great Hucklow and Little Hucklow, Wardlow and Foolow. The parish extended beyond Stoke Hall and Nether Padley to the east and encompassed the towns of Buxton, Tideswell and Chapel-en-le-Frith. However, in the nineteenth century the parish was much reduced in size when the separate parishes of Bradwell, Edale and Fairfield were created. In 1841 the census return showed that the Parish of Hope had 4,434 inhabitants in a total area of 36,160 acres.

The village of Hope was once part of a Royal Hunting Reserve and there is ample evidence to this effect in the church which contains ancient memorials bearing the symbols of forest officers, who were known as Woodroffes. The term survived as a family name for more than 500 years, and there is still a hostelry in the village called the Woodroffe Arms.

Bearing the same unchanged name for over 1,000 years now, the village is one of the oldest settlements in the immediate vicinity. Indeed, there are still records surviving from a charter dated AD 926 which record the victory in a nearby battle of King Athelstan, the first King of England and grandson of Alfred the Great. Athelstan went on to buy land at both Ashford and Hope.

The church has many treasures of historical significance, including a carved oak pulpit which dates from 1652 and a schoolmasters chair dating from the same period. Also, a rare Geneva Bible, or 'Breeches Bible' is displayed on one of the walls, wherein reference is made to Adam and Eve wearing 'breeches' rather than 'aprons'. There are also some quaint traditions which were instituted in earlier times; the vicar's wife received an annual payment of 10s – remuneration for washing the vicar's surplice. Also, at the conclusion of every marriage service the parish clerk uttered the words 'God speed you weel'. There was another custom practised at wedding ceremonies, which was to place a rope across the church door in order that, as the couple were preparing to leave, an exit toll could be demanded. Another custom practised by the residents of Hope, was their right to dig peat on the Crookstone Moorland, but it has been many years since this right was exercised.

In 1882 the chancel of the church was entirely rebuilt, and then in 1908, the east end of the chancel was again rebuilt. At that time, the east window was enlarged, and a stone screen and marble reredos behind the altar were erected. Much of the new wood carving introduced at the time was the work of local craftsman, the late Mr Micah.

Most of the stained glass in St Peter's church dates from the twentieth century with two significant exceptions – the armorial shields, bearing the arms of Eyre quartering Padley, and those of Gell of Hopton. A series of windows in the chancel represents events of the Passion and the Resurrection of Our Lord. St Peter, the church's patron saint, figures prominently in many of these windows. The series of five windows were designed and manufactured by the company of the late Mr C. E. Kempe. The period between 1906 and 1908 saw further additions. The Vicar at that time, the Revd E. C. Vincent, gave the two windows which can be seen on the south side of the chancel. The east window and the two smaller windows on the north side of the chancel were presented by Mr E. Willoughby Firth. There are two windows in the north aisle; the window above the altar represents the Annunciation and was the gift of Mr and Mrs Henry Freckingham. The window in the north wall, the gift of the late Mrs Vincent, represents the Nativity of Our Lord. The window in the south aisle, the Deliverance of St Peter out of prison by the Angels, is by Messrs C. E. Kempe and Co., and was the gift of Miss Annie Middleton. A small window in the west wall of the tower, donated in commemoration of the late Mr Joseph Nicholson, represents the Draught of Fishes.

Some of the stones which formed part of the village stocks, have been built into the churchyard wall and can be seen close to the north gate facing Edale Road.

A ninth-century Saxon preaching cross – similar to those at Eyam and Bakewell – along with an old Market Cross, stand on either side of the path on the southern side of the church.

Directly opposite to the old Blacksmiths Cottages in Hope, at the junction of Pindale Road and Castleton Road, is the Woodroofe Arms. The inn was built on land belonging to the family. The Woodroofes of Hope were the King's Foresters of The Peak and fought at Agincourt where they gained a Grant of Arms. The family name is derived from the title of 'Wood-Reeve' and dates from the reign of Edward IV. Members of the Woodroofe family continued as innkeepers and parish clerks for many generations. Nicholas Woodroofe was parish clerk at the time of his death in 1628, then Thomas Woodroofe in 1667, followed by Nathan Woodroofe in 1676. Although there was a short break in the family tradition, the accounts show that Ellis Woodroofe was clerk in 1710; and, upon his death in 1731, he was succeeded by his son Nathan, who, in turn was succeeded by his son, another Nathan Woodroofe. The Woodroofe family held the office of parish clerk for more than 200 years, and kept the inn until 1854.

At the end of Station Road stands the sixteenth-century Hall Hotel, which from 1720 until 14 September 1876 was known as the Cross Daggers Inn, because of the fact that travellers in cutlery coming from Sheffield stayed at the hostelry on their way to the cities of Liverpool and Manchester. Another popular venue is the Cheshire Cheese Inn on Edale Road. Legend has it that the inn served as an overnight stop on the old salt carrying route from Cheshire over the Pennines to Yorkshire and that traders paid for their lodging in rounds of Cheshire cheese!

Hope Wakes Week is traditionally held towards the end of June, close to the Patronal Festival of St Peter on 29 June, when the ancient Derbyshire tradition of well dressing is observed.

The Agricultural Shows in Hope date back to 1853. In 1944, the Hope Sheep Dog Club was formed in order to provide support for the Red Cross in the Second World War. In later years it combined with the Agricultural Society. The show takes place on August Bank Holiday Monday every year.

Today the village has a population of almost 900 inhabitants, and has many shops, cafés and other amenities serving both the local population and Hope's many visitors. The valley is a haven for walkers, rock climbers, bikers and pony trekkers. Many other activities are followed in the valley, such as bird watching, angling and painting, not to mention the increasingly popular sport of potholing. Over at the head of the valley,

Mam Tor is used as a launching pad for hand gliders, although it served a very different purpose in former times, when Iron Age man built a fort at the hill's summit.

Tideswell

Tideswell lies in a wide, dry valley on a limestone plateau, some seven miles north-east of Buxton in the Derbyshire Peak District, and about eighteen miles south-west of Sheffield. Eyam is five miles from Tideswell. In former days, Tideswell was a thriving market town; a town where the 'Great Courts' of the Royal Forest of the Peak were held in the time of Edward I. The town's fourteenth-century parish church has been described as being one of the county's most important medieval churches; also, one of Derbyshire's oldest schools was founded in Tideswell.

The town's wealth was built upon lead mining and the wool trade. Later, in the post-medieval period, silk weaving, cotton doubling, velvet and fustian cutting and the more traditional industries of limestone quarrying, stone-masonry and dry-stone walling assumed greater significance in the town's increasing prosperity and economy. Indeed, there is still a strong residual tradition of craftsmanship within the town. However, the fact that Tideswell was not served by a direct rail link, coupled with the growth of larger industrial towns and cities in the region, ultimately lead to the decline of many of the town's industries and the continued prosperity of the town itself. Today Tideswell, which is now a quiet upland village of great charm and some considerable character, offers much to interest tourists, having a fascinating history and many remarkable buildings, but the most notable event is undoubtedly the annual week-long Wakes Festival; a village tradition for well over 700 years. The Wakes Festival coincides annually with Tideswell well dressing which takes place on the Saturday nearest to the 24 June – the church's Patronal Festival Day. The culmination of the festival is the torchlight procession, lead by a brass band playing the 'Tideswell Processional'.

Tideswell can be justifiably proud of winning both the Derbyshire Best Kept Village Award and the East Midlands section of the Britain in Bloom Contest on several occasions. Locally, the town is called 'Tidza' or 'Tidsa' and the townsfolk are known as 'Sawyeds'. The story is told of a farmer whose cow got its head stuck in a farm gate. In order to free the cow, the farmer did no more than saw off its head! The story is still re-enacted by a local mummers group called the Tidza Guisers.

On a visit to the town in 1790, the Hon. John Byng wrote that 'At Tiddswell I stopt at a comfortable public-house, The New George, where being instantly served with cold roast beef and pigeon-pye, I felt very contented'. The coaching inn, built in 1730, is still trading, although the prefix 'New' is no longer used, and 'pigeon pye' is not on the menu!

It is often said that Tideswell is 'too big to be a village and too small to be town'. For the last 200 years the population has remained relatively static at around 2,000 souls.

There is ample evidence, from both place names and also the Domesday Book, that there was a settlement at Tideswell before the Norman Conquest. The place name itself is a conjunction of 'Tidi', who was a Saxon chieftain in the region, and the Mercian word, wælla, meaning stream. When the Domesday survey was conducted, Tiddeswall (as it was now known) was a berewick of the Royal Manor of Hope, which, in itself, was part of the king's estates. The entry is recorded in the Domesday Book as follows:

In Hope, with the outliers Edale, Aston, Shatton, half of Offerton, Tiddeswall, Stoke, Muchedeswelle, King Edward had 10 c. of land taxable. Land for 10 ploughs. Now 30 villagers and 4 smallholders have 6 ploughs. A priest and a church, to which belongs 1 c. of land. 1 mill, 5s 4d; meadow, 30 acres; woodland pasture in places 4 leagues and 2 furlongs long and 2 leagues wide.

Before 1066 these three manors paid £30, 5½ sesters of honey and 5 wagon-loads of 50 lead sheets; now they pay £10 6s. William Peverel has charge.

The three manors are Bakewell, Ashford and Hope.

The Peverels continued to hold the manor for three generations, until Henry II confiscated their estates. The manor was granted to Thomas Armiger or Lameley in 1207 by King John. Thomas's daughter married Paulinus de Brampton. In the late thirteenth century the manor was sold to Richard Daniel. When his grandson died without a male heir, the manor passed to his three daughters, but by the early fifteenth century the manor was owned by the Meverill family.

In 1251 Paulinus de Brampton was granted a charter to hold a weekly market in Tideswell every Wednesday. The charter also granted that a fair could be held between 23 June and 25 June. However, it was not until 1393 that the weekly market was confirmed and the dates of the annual fair changed to 28 August and 29 August.

During the time of the plague at Eyam, when entrance to the fair was controlled by the parish constable keeping watch and ward at the eastern entrance to the town, a woman from Eyam gained entry by deception. She was later recognised as being from Eyam and promptly pursued and driven from the town.

With a flourishing economy and population, the weekly markets continued to grow throughout the post-medieval period, and by the latter half of the eighteenth century there were three fairs being held annually; 3 May for cattle, the first Wednesday in September for sheep and cattle, and 18 October also for sheep and cattle.

By 1846 the number of fairs had increased to five, with the last two being particularly important for the sale of cheese, in addition to cattle and sheep. Following the Enclosure Award of 1822, parcels of land at the northern end of the town were allocated to be used specifically for the annual fairs; a two-acre plot at Town Head for sheep and a four-acre site at Wheston Bank for cattle fairs.

Much of modern Tideswell is constructed around the Market Place but the market itself, alas, no longer operates.

Without any doubt, Tideswell's most prominent and significant building was constructed just to the east of the Market Place, the magnificent fourteenth-century Parish Church of St John the Baptist, known as The Cathedral of The Peak. However, it is known that there was a chapel at Tideswell as early as 1192, when King John bestowed on the Bishop of Lichfield and Coventry the church of Hope and its chapel at Tideswell. But, by 1232, the church at Tideswell had become independent of Hope, being, by that time, a parish in its own right and having its own vicar. By the licence of Edward III, Sir John Foljambe founded a chantry, for two priests to say mass at St Mary's altar within the church. This was later confirmed by Richard II in 1383. The chantry became associated with a guild, such that two chaplains were to pray for 'the Brethren and Sisters of the Gild of the Blessed Mary'. The present church replaced the earlier Norman chapel, being built between approximately 1320 and 1386. Because of the ravages of the Black Death which was sweeping the country, building work was delayed for some considerable time and only recommenced in 1346; finally being completed some fifty years later, the church has now dominated the skyline for over 600 years with its outstanding pinnacled tower. It is thought that the building of the church was commissioned by Sir John Foljambe, a member of a prominent local landowning family, although it was the wealth generated by the wool trade and lead mining industry which funded much of the construction – Tideswell-being a major centre for the lead-mining industry from medieval times to the nineteenth century.

In essence, the classically designed cruciform church has two main styles – the transepts, nave and aisles are from the late Gothic period, whilst the chancel and pinnacled tower, which was the last part of the church to be constructed, are in the newly-fashionable Perpendicular style. The spacious church has a great arch of stunning proportions, with the chancel having a number of tall, traceried, clear-glass windows, often described as being 'one gallery of light and beauty'. It is often stated, with much justification, that the parish church is the Peak's most perfect church.

The church has many treasures inside, including brasses, stained-glass windows and fine wood carvings, which are a fitting testimony to the unique skills of Advent Hunstone. Advent's talents were first observed by Canon Andrew, Vicar of Tideswell and Headmaster of the Grammar School in 1864. After some initial negotiations with Advent, he was installed in the vicarage coach-house and started working for 4 pence an hour. It was also the canon who encouraged Advent to transfer his talents from stone masonry to wood carving. Amongst many objects, which can still be admired in the church today, are the north transept screen, the lectern, the communion table, the vicar's chair, the reredos, the south door and the organ case. Hunstone's work can also be seen on the pew ends which have intricate carvings showing the sacraments; baptism, confirmation, communion, marriage, absolution, ordination and the last rites. The family tradition of wood carving continued after Advent's death for further generations; his son, Advent Jnr crafted the churchyard gates.

St John's, which is a Grade I listed building, has many significant memorials including some of the finest brasses in the Peak; there is a brass to Bishop Robert Pursglove, depicted in pre-English Reformation vestments. Bishop Pursglove was a great benefactor to the village of his birth and the founder of Tideswell's Royal Grammar School. He died in 1579. Another fine brass commemorates Sir John Foljambe. There is also a brass commemorating Sir Robert Lytton, of nearby Litton.

There is an altar tomb in the middle of the Chancel in which lies Sir Samson Meverill, 1388–1462; it is believed that he was one of the victors of Agincourt. The church also has two chapels in the south transept. In the Lytton chapel, there is the tomb of Robert Lytton and his wife Isabel. There is also the impressive Bower chapel which has the tomb of Sir Thurstan de Bower and his wife Margret. The tower screen, dating from 1904, is by John Oldrid Scott. The church also has two pipe organs – the main one, built by Forster and Andrews of Hull, dates from 1895 while the other organ, the chancel organ, dates from 1979.

A major restoration of St John's was embarked upon in 1875 and, as a result, in 'Churches and Chapels in The County of Derby' Rawlins described the church as being 'without exception the most perfect and beautiful specimen of pointed architecture to be found in the County, – or perhaps in any other parish church of its size in the entire Kingdom'. Sir John Betjeman described the church as being 'a grand and inspiring church of the fourteenth century'. Perhaps the most significant of the stained-glass windows is the east window, by Heaton, Butler and Bayne of Nottingham, which depicts the Tree of Jesse. The window dates from the time of the church's restoration.

Samuel Slack, who was born in the village in 1757, was a bass singer of some repute. He sang before George III. When auditioning to be a chorister at Cambridge, there was a stunned silence after his performance. None of the other would-be choristers felt able to follow such a bravura performance. Singer Slack was held in such high esteem that he was invited to lead the choir at Westminster Abbey. However, he declined, preferring the camaraderie of singing with his friends in the village.

The tale is told that following a degree of over-indulgence, at one of the town's many hostelries, Slack lay in a field to 'sleep it off'. However, his slumbers were soon curtailed by a snorting bull which he found looking down upon him. Immediately regaining his senses, Slack jumped up and issued an ear-piercing yell together with some well chosen expletives at the startled bull. This had the effect of frightening the animal, which immediately turned tail and ran off!

The Tideswell Royal Grammar School was founded and endowed by Bishop Robert Pursglove, in 1559, and stands immediately behind the parish church. Also located in the same area, are the Georgian Eccles Hall and Blake House; both buildings were acquired by the school. Eccles Hall, built in the first half of the eighteenth century, was used as a residence for the headmaster and accommodation for boarding pupils. Blake House, another notable Georgian building, provided additional accommodation for staff and pupils.

Pursglove was a native of Tideswell, and became Archdeacon of Nottingham and later Bishop of Hull. He was relieved of this appointment in 1560, when he refused to take the Oath of Supremacy. However, during the previous year, 1559, he had obtained Letters Patent from Queen Elizabeth to found a school in Tideswell. The deeds of foundation are dated as being 18 June 1560.

The original school building was replaced in 1742, and an upper storey was added in 1824. The school was a centre of learning for some 370 years, during which time many boys from the neighbourhood and some who were boarders, received an education. Included in that number was the son of the Revd Thomas Stanley, who, after finishing his education at Cambridge, became one of the masters of the school.

When the school closed its doors to pupils in 1927, the 'Robert Pursglove Educational Foundation' provided a Central School in Tideswell for boys and girls over eleven years of age. In addition, the fund provided Scholarships to Secondary Schools, and the 'Pursglove Dole', or 'Grammar School Dole' as it is known locally, continues to support poorer families in the district.

CATHERINE MOMPESSON'S FAVOURITE WALKS

Walk to Boundary Stone

Leaving the rectory, Catherine would immediately turn left and head towards the Square – a walk of about half a mile. From there it is but a short walk to the Causeway where, to the left, the family butcher's of George Siddall & Daughters can be seen. Crossing the road, you will see, directly ahead of you, the lane which leads to Lydgate and the graves of George Darby and his daughter, Mary. The Lydgate Graves, as they are known, are a bit further on to the right, about another half mile from the Square. The enclosure, which is not consecrated ground, contains two lichen-covered grave stones; that of George Darby and his young daughter, Mary. The ground is sacred to the memory of father and daughter and states: 'Here lye buried George Darby, who died July 4 1666; Mary the daughter of George Darby, died September 4 1666.'

Departing the graves, continue along the narrow lane which leads to a forked junction; the left-hand fork is a footpath, Mill Lane, leading to Stoney Middleton and the right-hand fork is another footpath which also leads to Stoney Middleton, but via the Boundary Stone. From this point, the Boundary Stone is approximately one mile distant. So, taking the right-hand footpath, continue past a number of cottages on the left, to a gateway which gives onto a narrow footpath – a footpath which Catherine Mompesson would doubtless have walked along on many occasions. The narrow footpath then leads to a kissing gate and then to open moorland. This common land is where many pest houses were built to both isolate and accommodate parishioners who moved away from the village during the time of the plague. There are majestic views from here, to both the left and right. Upon reaching the Boundary Stone, observe the six drilled holes

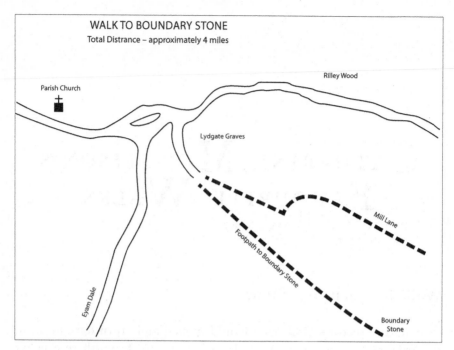

Walk to the Boundary Stone.

in the top surface of the stone, wherein coins were placed in exchange for provisions and medicaments, which had been deposited by people from nearby villages and hamlets. At the time of the plague, the holes were filled with vinegar in the belief that, by washing the coins, they would be purified from the 'seeds of the plague'. Return to Eyam via the same route in reverse.

Walk to Bretton

Fittingly, we start our walk from the parish church of Saint Lawrence, which was known during the Revd Mompesson's day as the church of Saint Helen. In the churchyard we can see the tomb of Catherine Mompesson and also the ancient Saxon Cross. Leaving by the west side gate, we immediately come to the so-called Plague Cottages which are located to our right. The first cottage is where the Hawksworth family lived – Peter Hawksworth being the third victim of the plague. The next cottage is where George Viccars died on 7 September 1665; he was the first victim of the plague. On the other side of the road, directly opposite, is Bagshaw House; this was the home of Emmott Syddall – she was betrothed to Rowland

Torre from Stoney Middleton but she died on 29 April 1666. Eight other members of Emmott's family died during the plague. Next door to the plague cottage is Rose Cottage, which is where the Thorpe family lived; they also suffered tragic losses at the time of the plague.

Walking further on, we come to the Brick House which was once an inn called the Stag's Parlour. The Brick House had not been built when Catherine lived in the village. We're now nearing the area in the village known as the Cross, which is where the village stocks were and also the market hall – a place where Catherine would visit on a regular basis. Opposite to this is the imposing structure of Eyam Hall, which Catherine would not have known as it was only completed after she had met her death. Immediately past Eyam Hall on the left is Eyam Close, which leads to Cucklett Delph, where Mompesson held his services of Divine Worship throughout much of the period of the plague. Our walk then takes us past the post office, which is on our right, and on as far as Hawkshill Road where we'll come back into the village at the end of our walk. Moving up the slight brew, we pass the site of Bradshaw Hall which is on the right, before coming to the old Royal Oak, which is also situated on the right. Bradshaw Hall was built by Francis Bradshaw but was demolished in the eighteenth century. Part of the building was subsequently used as a cotton mill. The Bradshaw family left the village in 1660, before the outbreak of the plague, and never returned on a permanent basis.

Immediately after passing the Royal Oak, which was for many years one of the village hostelries, we come to the home of Humphrey Merrill now known as Merrill Cottage. Catherine must have often visited this property, as Humphrey Merrill was the local apothecary; he died of the plague on 9 September 1666, but his wife, Anne, survived. One of Humphrey Merrill's relatives, Andrew Merrill, spent some time in a hut on Eyam Moor, isolated from the village and, by taking this action, he thus managed to avoid the ravages of the plague.

Continuing up the road, we come to West End Cottage on the left which is where the Wilson family lived and, like so many other families in the village, most of their number were struck down by the pestilence. A little further along, and looking up Tideswell Lane, is the cottage which was owned by the self-appointed plague sexton, Marshall Howe. Immediately on the left of Tideswell Lane there is the Townhead factory. This building would not have been known to Catherine, as the factory was only built in 1735 as a silk-weaving mill. Leaving Town Head, there is a slight brew which takes us out of Eyam. A little way from here we come to Eyam View Farm, which is just less than a mile from our starting point. The road continues to rise as we head out on the Foolow road, until we reach the peak by the sign for the Fine Grinding (Fluorspar) Ltd on the right.

We now have a short downhill section which takes us to Shepherd's Flatt farm. This is a farm which Catherine would have visited on many occasions, as the Morten family lived here and they too lost many members of their family during the visitation of the distemper. The Kempes were another family living at Shepherd's Flatt and they also suffered much distress during the time of the plague. Shepherd's Flatt farm is now a Caravan Club site. The farm is a little more than one mile from Eyam View farm. The next significant point is the Bull's Head Inn at Foolow, which is another half mile from Shepherd's Flatt farm. Foolow was part of the parish of Eyam, when William Mompesson was rector. The Bull's Head Inn at Foolow obtained a licence to sell spirits under The Sale of Spirits (or Gin) Act in 1753. The Foolow village cross dates from the fourteenth century and was removed to its present position on the village green in 1868 from the Wesleyan Reform Chapel.

Leaving the hamlet of Foolow, where many people died during the plague, we pass Saint Hugh's church on our right and take the road signposted, Bretton, which is also on the right. We walk along Bagshaw Lane and out into open countryside with Eyam Edge straight ahead of us, with our road clearly delineated as we steadily climb towards the Barrel Inn. Originally a farmhouse, dating from the late sixteenth century, it opened its doors as an inn as early as 1753 – an ideal location for an inn, as the bridle path from Hathersage to Eyam met here as did the road from Sheffield to Buxton. The inn derived its name because extensive mining in the area, for lead, fluorspar and barytes, created many deep caverns, including one which was barrel-shaped – hence the name, Barrel Inn!

As we reach the top of the hill we can see the Sir William Hill television mast, marking one of the highest points in Derbyshire. This is perhaps the longest stretch on our walk, and maybe also the steepest, as we walk on a steady incline, almost as soon as leaving the hamlet of Foolow. Bradshaw Lane continues to the right until the tiny hamlet of Bretton is reached, when one of the oldest and highest pubs in Derbyshire comes into view. The Youth Hostel is signposted to the right, and the Barrel Inn is on the left. The car park, which is immediately to the front of the inn, gives superb views of the surrounding countryside and also a commanding view of Shepherd's Flatt farm immediately below. The inn is situated at the dividing line between the light and the dark peak. Looking down to the right we see the hamlet of Foolow, through which we've just passed. The distance from Foolow to the Barrel Inn is a little more than one mile.

Walking towards the crest of the hill there is a public footpath signpost on the right which directs us back towards the village of Eyam, but our path takes us over the crest and onwards to Highcliffe. We make the final short climb to the summit, keeping to the main road. After the summit, we

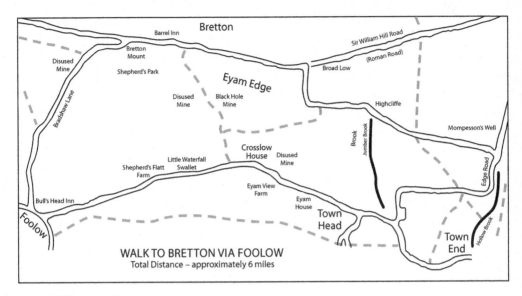

Walk to the Bretton.

drop down a little to Highcliffe. There is another footpath marked here, which also leads down to the village of Eyam via Jumber Brook. There are excellent views over the village and the quarries, to our right, as we drop into the hamlet. Continuing, we walk along the road until we reach the junction with Edge Road. We've now walked a further mile and a half from the Barrel Inn. At the junction which is signposted Grindleford to the left and Eyam to the right, turn left and walk up the brew until seeing the inlet on the left marked Mompesson's Well. Having viewed the well, turn and return to the junction, carry straight on, and then follow the Edge Road down until coming to Hawkshill Road. Generally, there isn't too much traffic along this section, but it pays to keep vigilant and also to the right-hand side of the road, facing any on-coming traffic. There are good views of the village to the left, as we are still at quite a height. We pass the youth hostel on our right and then, after having walked down a further half a mile, we come into Hawkshill Road, passing the public car park on the left and Eyam Museum on our right. At the bottom of Hawkshill Road we turn left and we're back on the main street. We head back into the village itself and towards our starting point of the church. The distance from Edge Road junction to the church is just less than a mile.

Available from June 2012 from Amberley Publishing

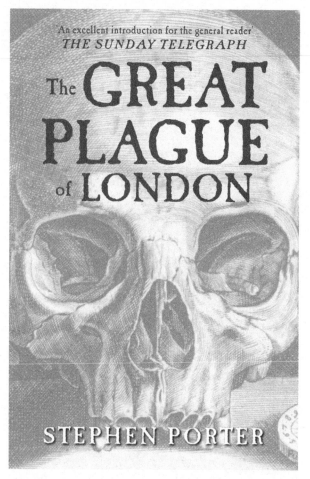

'An excellent introduction for the general reader'
THE SUNDAY TELEGRAPH

The bubonic plague epidemic which struck England in 1665-6 was responsible for the deaths of almost a third of London's population. Its sheer scale was overwhelming and it was well-recorded, featuring in the works of Pepys and Defoe and described in terrible detail in the contemporary Bills of Mortality. Stephen Porter describes the disease and how people at the time thought it was caused. He gives details of the treatments available (such as they were) and evokes its impact on the country. We will probably never know the reasons for the disappearance of the bubonic plague from England after 1665. What is clear is the fascination the subject still holds.

£10.99 Paperback
61 illustrations
192 pages
978-1-4456-0773-6

Available from June 2012 from all good bookshops or to order direct
Please call **01453-847-800**
www.amberleybooks.com